The Land of My Misfortunes
Vietnam, America, and The Book of Genesis

Conversations About Faith and War

Moderated by Alan Cutter

Edited by Ann Cutter

Copyright © 2018 Alan Cutter

All rights reserved.

ISBN-13: 978-1985793804
SBN-10: 1985793806

*To my companions on the journey
remembering with fondness
those who participated in this conversation*

Scripture Quotations are from the
New Revised Standard Version of the Bible
Copyright © 1989 National Council of Churches of Christ
in the United States of America.
Used by permission. All rights reserved.

Alan Cutter

CONTENTS

	About the Moderator	vii
1	Foreword	1
2	Introduction	Pg 6
3	Creation and Battle	Pg 9
4	Called to Service	Pg 39
5	Sacrifice	Pg 72
6	Apocalypse: Then and Now	Pg 99
7	Darkness and Dreams	Pg 124
8	Home?	Pg 147
9	More About the Moderator	Pg 170

About the Moderator

Alan is a retired Presbyterian pastor. He is also a Vietnam veteran, a disabled veteran, living with post-traumatic stress disorder (PTSD) and Agent Orange related Parkinson's disease.

The PTSD came first. With the help of counselors at VET Centers and companions in a veterans' organization, and with the support of a wonderful and compassionate congregation in Duluth, Minnesota, Alan confronted that diagnosis and determinedly claimed his life, recognizing that PTSD and the trauma of war would always be a part of who he was.

In 2010, Veterans Administration doctors diagnosed Alan with Parkinson's disease. In one of those coincidences that astound us, his diagnosis came in the same month that Parkinson's disease was declared an Agent Orange "presumptive," that is to say, if one had "boots on the ground" and develops Parkinson's disease, it is assumed that Agent Orange is the cause and no further substantiation is required.

Alan had been able to work while living with PTSD, but the combination of Parkinson's disease and PTSD made it impossible for him to continue.

He retired a bit earlier than he had planned. The combination of the PTSD and the Parkinson's affects his ability to concentrate; it takes him a long time to complete tasks that he used to do rather quickly.

I hasten to add that his sense of humor and the ridiculous remains strong and his ability to make outrageous puns is as maddening as ever. His intellect and faith have not been shaken. He is not depressed about the Parkinson's disease; as he says, he went through all of that "emotional shit" with the initial diagnosis of PTSD and does not need to do it again, even if people think he should! We enjoy our children and grandchildren, traveling here and there to see friends and make new ones, and helping others, as we are able. Physically, Alan will tell people that he is slower moving and a little unsteady; he says he has one-cane days, two-cane days, and occasional no-cane days.

As part of his own process of continued healing, Alan often re-reads reflections and material he has helped create over the years as he was working through questions about trauma and faith, drawing strength and encouragement in recalling the journey of healing and hope he has taken. The transcribed conversations and their insights are too good not to share!

Ann (and Alan) Cutter
St. Petersburg, FL
2018

Foreword

This book contains transcriptions of conversations that were held in 1999, when the then National Conference of Viet Nam Veteran Ministers (later the International Conference of War Veteran Ministers) met for its Annual Conference. This organization was founded to give members an opportunity to tell and reflect upon their own stories of their time as warriors. As a participant on my own journey and wanting to explore further the intersection between the great stories of faith and my own experiences, I proposed a conference program of six structured conversations around parts of the Book of Genesis. Journalist Bill Moyers had recently held such conversations during a Public Television Series, *Genesis*, and I thought it would be interesting if we approached our experiences using these seminal stories as well. The group accepted my proposal.

The transcriptions that you will read have only been lightly edited for some clarity and to remove information that would involve the names or identities of people whose relationship to the conversation was in the realm of "this person was there as well." Transcribing conversations is tricky; pauses are common while thoughts are gathered, and at times the thoughts change in mid-stream. There is a lot of jumping back and forth, as well as interrupting. Since punctuation can change meaning, the reader will find a liberal use of dashes.

All the participants were well aware that the conversations were being recorded as two tape recorders were on the coffee table in front of us. It was clearly understood that the material would be published at some time, though it has taken almost a decade to get around to it.

The participants are identified by first names only. If some person is truly curious, he or she can do some research and perhaps figure out the identities of "Phil" or "Jack" or "Linda." I am the "Alan" who acted as the moderator. New names have been given to a few individuals, though all conversations with a name reflect the thoughts of one person. Remember that what is important is the conversation.

We were a total of thirteen: a dozen religious professionals along with a layperson who came from a Jewish background but who had a deep interest in our mission of education, healing, and outreach. We were all, again with the exception of the layperson, individuals who had served in the Armed Forces, some in an enlisted capacity and others as officers, and who had been deployed in Vietnam, though at different times and in different places with a multitude of tasks. We represented Army, Navy, Marines, and Air Force. Four of the group had been Army chaplains, though one had been an enlisted man in Vietnam and only later became a chaplain. The theological perspective of the group ranged from liberal to conservative, and everything in between. However, the common elements that allowed us to converse were our shared experience of war and our deep respect for one another.

The impetus for these conversations about faith arose from the deep frustration we had experienced as we sought to engage our own denominations, religious communities, and supposed superiors in serious conversation about war, and the absolute refusal by these groups and individuals to even listen to what we had to say. These groups and leaders were committed to a couple perspectives.

One perspective could be summed up in the sentence, "I won my medals legit," an assertion which implies that is possible to serve "honorably" in a time of war. This reflects the point of view of what is commonly called the "just war" theory, which outlines certain criteria that, if met, allow one society to wage war against another, always within a set of accepted "rules." Oddly enough the belief in a set of "rules" which then define activities as honorable is also the foundation of the "peace church" movement. That movement takes as its foundation the "rule" of non-violence, valuing negotiations and compromise, listening and talking, as proper paths for conflict resolution. When these fail, adherents to the "peace church" value a witness of presence in the face of violence. So powerful can such a witness be that the leadership of any group, especially one including "just war" adherents within its number, may feel so threatened by this witness of presence that the "peace church" people are labeled as traitors.

From either side, "just war" or "peace church," there is a belief that somewhere there are indeed "rules of engagement" which, if followed, will earn an individual the sobriquet of "honorable." There are many groups that loudly proclaim, "If you keep the rule, the rule will keep you." The stumbling block for this viewpoint is that not everyone plays by the same "rules," or even by any "rules." The real tragedy of both these presentations is that human conflict is ultimately reduced to a "game" that has "rules," and which is played – win, lose, or draw. The manner in which the game is played then determines "honor," turning both human struggle and dignity into cheap commodities on the game board.

Now it is indeed possible to serve "honorably" according to the parameters above, and many have, and God bless them and may they be ever thankful that they happened to be in situations where the "rules" applied, and everyone more or less agreed upon the "rules." May their voices continue to be heard for such voices encourage us to evaluate the reality of our own experiences.

The second perspective advanced is summed up in the

sentence, "If you weren't there, you cannot understand!" If "honor" is earned by following the "rules," an agreed upon set of criteria which define behavior, then this perspective would allow for "no honor," for it asserts there are no real "rules" in war, or in life. This perspective proclaims that the "rules" exist, but then fearfully recognizes that this proclamation is a lie, and encourages action in such a way as to circumvent whatever "rules" have been asserted. Indeed, rewards and victory go to those who can best proclaim the lie while bending, breaking, and ignoring the "rules." This reflects the practical reality of actions of all the mainline churches in America regarding wars.

Since the reality of "no rules" is at odds with the "proclamation" the only way to maintain the "proclamation" is to silence the reality, thus allowing for the restoration of the "proclamation." Only those who have participated know the reality, and they are not allowed to talk about it! It is the hiddenness of the unspeakable truth of the chaos around the corner. After all, the absence of "rules" is the presence of chaos, and to talk of chaos is extremely uncomfortable. The stumbling block for this viewpoint is that chaos keeps breaking into life.

Even when the power of chaos keeps breaking through, it is acknowledged in only two ways: that (1) to speak of it as "good" for a society or for individuals to acknowledge this state where "we" are not, but "others" are; and that, if we did encounter chaos, we are glad "we" either avoided the chaos or found our way out and were restored to our former state; or (2) to speak of chaos as "bad," for then everyone coming out of it appears "crazed," and, since it doesn't seem to work to appear "crazed, in the world of the "proclamation" or lie, one must hide the "crazed" reality in order to be restored to the community. The real tragedy of this viewpoint is that one is more valued if one is perceived as sane, yet a liar, rather then as crazed, but a truth-teller.

Neither of these perspectives is very satisfactory, comforting, or helpful to those who have been in a war zone or involved in a traumatic incident.

I would suggest a perspective that has journeyed through the "just war" theory and "peace church" movement with their emphasis on justice; then made a stop at the "proclamation" way station, inhaled the lie and its emphasis on restoration; and gone on to a new territory with some different assumptions. This perspective assumes that there is order in creation, but not in humanity; admiring the natural order only makes obvious the human disorder. Accepting then that the basic state of human relationships always borders on the verge of chaos, one can then recognize how simple it is to tumble over the edge when something, say a war, disturbs the careful societal arrangements offered by the first two perspectives, which, let it be noted, form the basis for most of daily life and without which life would be unmanageable. However, this perspective has learned, and now recognizes, that chaos is just around the corner. Within the experience of chaos, or trauma, survival becomes the paramount objective, be it the survival of an individual or the survival of a society. Coming out of the trauma what one needs is neither "justice," nor "restoration," but "meaning," which is then defined in terms of integrity, compassion and transmission of the truth. This perspective is what I would advance. Incidentally the emphasis in this perspective is not "justice" or "restoration," but the possibility of fullness of life for the whole person of an individual or, in our case, for wounded warriors.

What you will be reading will not be any formal Bible study which is based upon any definable principles of exegesis, or textual study or discernment. Instead what you will find is an exercise in **eisegesis**, a way that Scripture is read that allows one to link one's life directly to a story of faith using the Scripture to stimulate discussion. While exegesis is usually a detached study, looking at the Scriptures from a distance, thinking about and reflecting on the apothetic Creator (God far away from us), eisegesis invites us to an encounter with the katathetic Creator (God near to us). This encounter is, as you will see, much more personal.

As you read, do so with imagination so that you might hear the voices, feel the passion and the pain, and touch the yearning hope for the freedom to enjoy the promise and fullness of life.

Introduction
The Original Proposal

Introduction: Much reflection has been devoted to how a person of faith should respond to war; these reflections have generally been grouped around the two extremes of "just war theory" and pacifism, the outright intellectual endorsement of war and its brutality being too much for people of faith to accept, though people of faith have not hesitated to adopt such a stance as a matter of practice. For those of us attending the annual meeting of the National Conference of Viet Nam Veteran Ministers such reflections, while interesting, have little real meaning. For us such reflections are too late. We have been to war. We want to use our theological training to reflect upon the experience of war.

Goal: In conversation, at our annual meeting, using a variety of "windows," we will endeavor to reflect upon the experience of war using the resources of the sacred writings.

In 1999, we are using the resources of the Bible, particularly that book known as Genesis as a starting point for our discussions.

Objectives:
1. Provide a format for this Annual Conference meeting
2. Focus thoughts about our experiences and our callings

3. Share our reflections as a resource to the larger community

Process: For the 1999 Conference we will have six sessions of approximately one hour to one and a half hours during which we will have conversations using themes and stories suggested by the book of Genesis. These conversations will be recorded and transcribed and offered for publication with minor editing. **Participants should be aware of this before the conversations begin and be willing to participate.** Participants will be reminded that the conversation is being taped. The assumption is that those participating will be familiar with each other's stories, but that the stories are not the focus of the conversation. (<u>Members not wishing to participate may observe, and then offer their reflections and thoughts after each recording session is finished.</u>) Prior to the meeting notice of the relevant passages will be provided, as well as the general focus for discussion. Note that when we proceed to publish our conversations Biblical references and summaries will be based upon the New Revised Standard Version of the Bible.

There is no intention that we would reach any conclusion or even agreement; only that we would hold conversation and explore together the interaction between our experiences and the Scripture (or other sacred writing).

Session 1: Creation & Battle
    Genesis 1 & 2: the two stories of creation
    Genesis 4: Cain and Abel
Focus: The connection between the IMAGO DEI and the essence of war

Session 2: Called to Service
    Genesis 12 & 13: Abram & Sarah
    Focus: The experience of being summoned to service

Session 3: Sacrifice
    Genesis 22 & 23: Abraham & Isaac
    Focus: What we were called to do – who killed who?

Session 4: Apocalypse Then & Now
    Genesis 6 – 8: Noah and the flood
    Focus: Who survived, why, and how? Is survival worth it?

Session 5: Darkness & Dreams
    Genesis 28 – 32: Jacob wrestling
    Focus: The dark night of the soul & hope

Session 6: Home?
    Genesis 39-40: Joseph in Egypt
    Focus: Where is the warrior's home? An exile forever?

The Land of My Misfortunes
Vietnam, America, and the Book of Genesis

Creation and Battle

Excerpts from Genesis, chapters, 1,2, and 4 (NRSV)

Then God said, "Let us make humankind in our image, according to our likeness; and let them have dominion over the fish of the sea, and over the birds of the air, and over the cattle, and over all the wild animals of the earth, and over every creeping thing that creeps upon the earth." So God created humankind in his image, in the image of God he created them; male and female he created them. God blessed them and God said to them, "Be fruitful and multiply, and fill the earth and subdue it; and have dominion over the fish of the sea and over the birds of the air and over every living thing that moves upon the earth." God said, "See, I have given you every plant yielding seed that is upon the face of the earth. And every tree with seed in its fruit; you shall have them for food. And to every beast of the earth, and to every bird of the air, and to everything that creeps upon the earth, everything that has the breath of life, I have given every green plant for food." And it was so. God saw everything that he had made, and indeed, it was very good...

* * * * *

Then The Lord God formed man from the dust of the ground, and breathed into his nostrils the breath of life; and the man became a living being. And the Lord God planted a garden in Eden, in the east; and there he put the man whom he had formed. Out of the ground the Lord God made to grow every tree that is pleasant to the sight and good for food, the tree of life also in the midst of the garden, and the tree of the knowledge of good and evil . . . . The Lord God took the man and put him in the garden of Eden to till it and keep it. And the Lord God commanded the man, "You may eat freely of every tree in the garden, but of the tree of the knowledge of good and evil you shall not eat, for in the day that you eat of it you shall die." Then the Lord God said, "It is not good that the man should be alone; I will make him a helper for a partner" . . . . So the Lord God caused a deep slumber to fall upon the man, and he slept; then he took one of his ribs and closed up its place with flesh. And the rib that the Lord God had taken from the man he made into a woman and brought her to the man. The man said, "This at last is bone of my bone and flesh of my flesh; this one shall be called Woman, for out of Man this one was taken."

* * * * *

Now the man knew his wife Eve, and she conceived and bore Cain, saying, "I have produced a man with the help of the Lord." Next she bore his brother Abel. Now Abel was a keeper of sheep and Cain a tiller of the ground. In the course of time Cain brought to the Lord an offering of the fruit of the ground, and Abel for his part brought of the firstlings of his flock, their fat portions. And the Lord had regard for Abel and his offering, but for Cain and his offering he had no regard. So Cain was very angry, and countenance fell. The Lord said to Cain, "Why are you so angry, and why has your countenance fallen? If you do well, will you not be accepted? And if you do not do well, sin is lurking at the door; its desire is for you, but you must master it."

Cain said to his brother Abel, "Let us go out into the field." And when they were in the field, Cain rose up against his brother Abel, and killed him. Then the Lord said to Cain, "Where is your brother Abel?" He said, "I do not know; am I my brother's keeper?"

And the Lord said, "What have you done? Listen; your brother's blood is crying out to me from the ground! And now you are cursed from the ground, which has opened its mouth to *receive your brother's blood from your hand. When you till the ground, it will no longer yield to you its strength; you will be a fugitive and wanderer upon the earth."*

Cain said to the Lord, "My punishment is greater than I can bear! Today you have driven me away from the soil and I shall be hidden from your face; I shall be a fugitive and wanderer on the earth; and anyone who meets me may kill me."

Then the Lord said to Cain, "Not so! Whoever kills Cain will suffer a seven-fold vengeance." And the Lord put a mark on Cain, so that no man who came upon him would kill him. Then Cain went away from the presence of the Lord, and settled in the land of Nod, east of Eden . . .

* * * * *

Participating: Alan, Charlie, Bruce, David, Ray, Jack, Jeff, John, Ken, Linda, Phil, Russ

* * * * *

Alan: As we reflect upon these stories of creation, which are rich with all kinds of imagery, and out of our experiences of our own nation and overseas, the first question I would ask you is what did creation look like? What did Eden look like?

Phil: It looked like a garden. It had lots of vegetation and animals, peace. Peaceful.

Alan: Peaceful?

Bruce: Probably like a greenhouse with a lot of mist. Maybe like a jungle without all the nasty stuff.

Alan: In other words, you think it was hot. It must have been if they were going around naked!

Bruce: Well, at least comfortable.

Linda: At least comfortable.

Phil: Humid.

Alan: There is a phrase here in this particular rendition of the creation story. It talks about Eden, calling it out in this way, "God planted a garden in Eden, in the east" - almost a land of pleasure in the east. Now if you think of the hot, humid garden being in the east, what did you think when you arrived in the east in the heat and humidity? Did you think that you arrived in Eden? What did you think when you arrived in Southeast Asia?

Ken: Heat; oppressive heat.

Phil: Stench.

Bruce: Hell.

Alan: Hell?

Bruce: I didn't know where I was. I was loaded on one of those C-130's. In the middle of the night I was whisked away from Okinawa and told once we got there where we were.

Jack: They didn't tell you it was Eden?

Russ: I thought my BOQ was temporary housing.

Alan What was it like?

Russ: Well, there were these insects that were large enough to eat your feet as you stepped in the shower. There was fungus growing out of the walls that looked as if it were carnivorous. Do I need to go on?

Alan: Go on. This is a marvelous description.

Ken: You had a shower?

Russ: There!

Ken: You had a building?

Charlie: I spent my first day in Nam in Camp Alpha. Such a

marvelous place. I thought I'd volunteer the Vietnamese to blow it up. But after the heat and the stench, the most memorable experience I had – well, I hadn't had a shower for three days. I went into the shower – I don't remember parts – but I just remember when the cleaning lady came in with the mop bucket. I thought, "This is the living end."

Jack: So you were naked in Eden?

Charlie: I was naked in Eden. Right.

Alan: And was it good. I mean it says here in the Scriptures that it was good.

Charlie: I think the sign on the walls said something about the "Water Is Not Potable."

Linda: Don't drink this!

John: The water was not [potable] there.

Charlie: I found this out later.

Jack: Alan, before you move to the next thing, I want to go back to the previous one where we had talked about the passage itself, and just look at it in the context of having been warriors, having gone overseas to impose our will on other people, which is the task of the military. In looking at this thing it really had never struck me before but here's part of the picture of Eden, "let them have dominion over the fishes of the sea," and so forth. And then God blessed them; God said to them go forth and multiply, fill the earth, subdue it – have dominion over the fishes of the sea. And I've gotten off on this picture of Adam and Eve, and instead of the old picture that I had of this land of delight where they didn't have to do anything, just kind of pick the bananas off the tree, and eat the fruits, and enjoy all the stuff with no responsibility – but they got responsibility – they got dominion – and I got this picture of Adam and Eve sitting down with a management manual trying to figure out what does it mean to have dominion over all this stuff? How do we organize the animals? How do we get the plants to grow? Because that's the task the have; it's almost as if Adam and Eve had been sent to Vietnam.

Alan: They had dominion.

Jack: Right. Had dominion.

Russ: Except in Vietnam it was dominion over people, and in there it's over other species.

Jack: O.K.

Linda: But that included other plants. Enough foliage was destroyed.

Alan: Then the image of God that we can get out of this particular passage of Scripture - that is, if we're made in the image of God – is that God has dominion over things, people, us. If so, is that what it means to be, to act, in the image of God? To enforce? To control? To dominate?

John: Well, how many times had God been used to kind of justify our way, that we are right. He's on our side, so "they" must be wrong.

Alan: "God blessed them and said to them. . ." Were we blessed before we went over?

David: Actually, cursed is what I remember.

Alan: Say more about that. What do you mean "cursed?"

David: Well, you see I graduated from the University of California at Berkeley in 1969. I had lots of people who knew I was in ROTC training at that time, and I never had anything real nice said to me about what I was going to do. I knew from the day I went on active duty I was going to Vietnam. That was in my active duty orders; so after a few brief interludes, I was on my way.

Alan: So you came out of the university where you'd been roundly cursed, went right into the military, which gave you a benediction and sent you overseas.

David: I wasn't remembering a benediction particularly.

Russ: That means a blessing!

David. I know that.

Jack: I'm thinking of some sayings of drill instructors and somehow "blessing" is a bit of stretch.

Alan: What sayings were you thinking of?

Jack: Uuhhh!

Alan: Go ahead. What have you got to lose? What's the worst that can happen to you? Are they going to send you back to Vietnam?

Jack: Actually it's just a string of expletives!

John: You could always sing a cadence song.

Bruce: "I don't know, but I've been told . . ."

David: "Eskimo's are pretty cool . . ."

John: One thing that I heard, though it wasn't told to me, a number of vets have recounted that every day they had to pray for war.

Alan: Had to pray for war. Because?

John: That was their job. That was what they were being trained to do. That was their job description.

Bruce: Who was praying for war?

John: The soldiers; they were marines. . .

Bruce: I hope it wasn't the drill sergeants because I missed that class.

John: This particular group.

Ken: I think we were blessed though by family, wives, husbands, friends; people sent us off with blessings and prayers that we would come back in one piece. It wasn't all curses and shouts.

Bruce: It's not a fair comparison anyway – Adam and Eve – because this is before the fall and now we are after the fall so we're a product of their sin. But we're talking about before they sinned, and this is the image of God, and the way they were made in the image of God is that they were given a conscience; they knew, they had the ability to know,

Linda: I don't know. I think they were pretty naïve in the start – about how lovely it was -- everything. At least in chapter one of Genesis the whole God image is at a distance. God wasn't present. In the other story God was right there breathing into the nostrils. But in this one God is distant and away and creating all this, so you get this image of "Oh, it's lovely and wonderful." So we, before the fall, before we arrived, we thought this is going to be [good]. Is there anyone who here that wasn't expecting something different from what we actually experienced?

Charlie: In Eden or in Vietnam?

Linda: Arriving in Vietnam.

Charlie: It was worse than I expected.

Phil: It was worse than I expected; I couldn't imagine it being that bad.

Charlie: I was scared witless to begin.

Phil: I remember when we were flying in helicopters how often we said that if there wasn't a war, this could be Eden. I remember hearing that. I remember saying that! It was so beautiful, all the vegetation; from the air, it was beautiful.

Charlie: Did Eden have mosquitoes and leeches?

David: It had warning signs. You saw one on the wall that said, "Don't drink the water." And this other says, "Don't eat from the tree." It may be Eden, but it's dangerous.

Alan: That's a good point. The same kind of danger sign we get here from the tree: from the tree of good and evil, "for the day you eat from it you shall die." You eat of the tree of the knowledge of good and evil.

Jack: So Eden is a place where if you do certain things you will die. It's not a totally safe place.

Russ: To take seriously what Bruce has said, by contrast, are we behaving by our search in this conversation to know good and evil? Is that kind of the contrast - you were saying we wouldn't be having such a conversation as this . . .

Bruce: If we didn't know the difference between good and evil.

Russ: But that's really how it's presented here. That Eden was before . . .

Bruce: They didn't know the difference between good and evil; they hadn't eaten of that tree yet.

John: Just like us.

Phil: Before that there was no evil. There was just pure goodness.

Bruce: The ambush was there; they had the choice to walk in or not.

Charlie: Evil was there.

Alan: Where was it?

Charlie: It was in the potential choice.

Phil: It was only potential evil – it wasn't real?

Charlie: Well, you hit that tripwire it becomes real evil. I'm stuck between reality and my Calvinist ancestors – did they have a choice? Was it really possible they weren't going to hit that tripwire?

John: The tripwire was when you went in the service. That's where you made that choice. There's no way you couldn't. You were going to Vietnam.

Jack: The fact that we see these parallels between Eden and the Vietnam experience, and granted that in the Genesis story there is THE FALL, I'm not sure that you can deduce from that [fall] that that fall was the only fall, because it was a paradigm, a prototype, a model of every fall that has taken place after that. And if you're drawing this analogy between Eden and Vietnam, Vietnam was really an American fall. There is an element in which we fell from grace in that experience.

Linda: I believe that evil was out there, sort of like that tree; it was out there. But once I was in Vietnam and I ate of that tree and it became part of me, I found out that I in fact had evil – that was the death of me, and that was the death of my Eden.

Charlie: Yes, it was the death of our innocence.

Jeff: You said much of what I would have said at that point. The innocence that we had – we may have thought we knew good and evil. We may have thought a lot of things. But hitting the ground and being faced with it full face, and at that point truly understanding what good and evil was, that was the death of innocence.

Linda: And again it was no longer out there; it was right here.

Ray: In many ways couldn't it be compared to having a parent, a spouse who is in the process of dying? You think you are prepared. You have been told all these things. But suddenly reality is in your face and you realize that you were not prepared to the extent that you might have been. At least for myself personally the first night was filled with lots of evil dropping all around us, and we were running around in our GI baggy, green skivvies with only "guns of pleasure" available for us, because the "guns of war" were locked up in Conex containers.

Alan: That's when you began to think about the war as evil? At that point? Or confusing?

Ray: I think that I was faced with the harsh reality of life versus death.

Ken: You know we were all young when we went over there – despite our chronological age, we were all young. And I always think of Adam and Eve as young until . . . and all of a sudden they got old, or older. We got old, like that. We didn't know it.

Linda: I was as old as I was ever going to get. And so much older than I ever expected to be.

Russ: You started with the idea of the text; well, the text was written considerably after the chronology that included Eden and the beginning, and so even the first readers of this passage, the first ones who wrote it down, were after the fall – whether it was a few years or several millennia – whoever wrote it down and first read it was involved in this business of knowing good and evil, or trying to figure it out.

Jack: Certainly if you took that thought to an even greater extreme and said somebody just made this thing up and wrote it down – a perspective that obviously a number of people here would disagree with – but even if you took that you can imagine the kind of probably "trauma experience" that would haunt "whoever" to make up this particular kind of story. There was a wonderful place. Something happened. Innocence was lost. The wonderful place was lost. We all aged. We all got tired. We all incorporated evil into ourselves. If this was written by someone who just made it up, it was someone who had gone through an experience we could all identify with, and agree with.

David: Perhaps Eden's not a place, but a state of being, of our innocence lost forever.

Alan: Can you identify a moment when it was lost – looking back? Is there any particular moment of arriving in-country or initial experience that all of a sudden you look around and said, "This is shit!"?

Phil: Well, it might be for me the first time that I really thought I wouldn't be going home. But that didn't happen the first day I got there. Not for me. It was somewhere in the middle. Because I really felt that I'd was going to be going home. But there was one point where I thought, "I may not be going home," and that is the time I think you age.

David: The one that stands out. It's a compound in Qui Nhon one night. I'm in my room. I had my own room. I shared it with a civilian from Australia who fixed cash registers for the PX – just to grind that thing in a bit more – but I'm in there. Suddenly everybody's alert around us and I'm not quite sure at that time what's going on; I later find out they had sappers in the compound. They wanted to knock off the PX I guess. I don't know. But they're in there, and I'm hearing noises outside. Now we didn't lock things up in the Conex box. We had our weapons with us; I has a .45 and a M-16, and a few other unauthorized items we won't go into. And I hear these noises outside the door of the room, so I'm ready. At the point, and the door comes open, because it wasn't locked. I didn't pull the trigger for some reason. If I had I would have blown away this 18-year-old kid from – I don't know where – but he's one of ours. But I had been hearing people say "They're inside; they're inside," and right then I could have killed a US soldier and that would have been the end of my innocence. It was the end of it anyway, even if I didn't. Just the prospect of what almost happened at that moment. That's when it went away for me.

Russ: A bit more about the text. This becomes for us an analogy. It may be fact in the whole scheme of total history but we read it as an analogy because we never were in Eden. We were in Vietnam, but we were not in Eden, even in our innocence whatever that amounted to. Our innocence has never been what Adam and Eve had. So when we read this we always read it as an analogy, and what I learn from looking at literature is that analogies are always imperfect. And so - I'm glad it's here – but the innocence of Eden is not something I have ever known. I wasn't born with it.

Bruce: No human being ever was.

Russ: And so to talk of this [Vietnam] as though it really is [or was Eden] is to kind of presume what we can't know.

Bruce: We never lost our innocence because we haven't been innocent.

Russ: And the reading of the innocence of Eden – we really can't know what the innocence might be – it's an imperfect analogy.

John: In retrospect to me, Phil, this country, before it went to war, felt like Eden to me. I felt I lost it. I could never get it back. I could never have the same appreciation.

Alan: The American Eden. The United States and Eden. What attributes did that Eden have?

John: Certainly Innocence.

David: Naiveté

John: Land of plenty.

David: A place where anything is possible. We can fix it. I felt like that.

Charlie: Some cautionary notes. In our youthful optimism we say "we're Americans." You guys say we can't do it. But we're Americans, we can do it.

David: We can fix all this.

Charlie: If we can do it, then you can do it too.

Ray: Just to take a step back from that though. I think of my first daughter standing on the third or fourth step of the stairway and simply leaping, knowing that I would catch her. Now that's innocence. It's a belief that the hand of her father is going to catch her and not allow harm to come to her. To me, that's complete innocence and faith in something much greater than what we are.

Bruce: That's why the Word says you can't enter the kingdom of God unless you come as a small child. That where we have to go to.

Jack: But after the kind of loss of innocence, of the experience of good and evil, that's been discussed around this table, how are you ever going to get back to that experience of a small child jumping into the arms of her father that Ray has just described?

Bruce: That what the cross is all about.

Jack. O.K.

Bruce: That's why Jesus died. To give us that opportunity to go back to that innocence – by giving our self up and crucifying our self. Not loving our life unto death,

Russ: I can understand that in one sense. But I've known of fathers that would call their children to do the very thing your daughter did who would purposely not catch their child so that they could alert them to the kind of world they live in. The Sidran Foundation, which focuses (in part) on domestic abuse, is attentive to a set of children as young as your daughter who found no such security in jumping into the hands of their fathers. So the story of the crucifixion and the Gospel story as is sometimes presented is very difficult, from experience, really to believe.

Bruce: And those fathers who would let their child fall are products of the fall! Back in the garden. Because there's certainly no perfect human father. No innocent human father because of the fall.

Russ: You're talking about me.

Bruce: Talking about you?

Russ: Yes.

Alan: There is another element in this section from Genesis as we talk about the creation story and read these particular words. Adam was alone until there was made a woman to be the helpmate. Linda, would you perhaps say something about how it felt to be an American woman in Vietnam?

Linda: I think one of the things that I've mentioned before is that women or girls grow up and then as women have the kind of innate instinct which is supportive of life, that we are caretakers, we are nurturers. So it really was as a helpmate; the idea was that we were going to support, connect with, be with our brothers – sometimes literally our brothers. I don't know what else to say about that. I guess part of it that was true was that we put ourselves second for many reasons in many situations for different people.

Alan: Those of us who were in country came in contact with a number of women at one point or another, for one reason or another. Charlie has talked us about the hooch maid coming in and cleaning up the shower, with the bucket. Think for a moment about the women in Vietnam – not only the Americans but also the Vietnamese. What is your thinking about the women in country?

Ken: Didn't trust them.

Alan: Didn't trust them? Why not?

Ken: I saw one pacing off the distance to the wire about the second day I was there. Going for a walk, measuring out for the mortars.

Phil: The few encounters with the women I had, they were mainly used as objects of sexual desire or lust, and after many days of jungle mission and we had a few days of stand down, if we had an opportunity to go for a quick R & R somewhere, that was what we did – at Vung Tao or Saigon – after buying some very expensive Saigon teas at five bucks a shot. Usually didn't get close until after you bought the third or fourth round.

John: You still bitter about that?

Jack: It's interesting in the Genesis story, the man and woman start out naked and something happens – the fall or whatever. After that thing happens, from then on for normal situations of men and women together, where respect is shown and humanity is shown between men and women, basically clothes are a sign of that respect and humanity. And the things that we've heard already that involve women and involve nakedness in Vietnam involve a disrespect for any shared humanity, a de-humanization. Charlie's story with the shower room – if you're of one sex and you walk into the room to clean while someone's taking a shower, basically what you doing is giving out the message "You're not here as a human being. Because if you were, I'd feel embarrassed. And I could care less. You're not a human being." And I was involved in the reverse of that; one day when I was in a jeep with two or three other Americans. We were driving down the road, came to a river, the day was hot, the situation was relatively peaceful; we weren't anticipating encountering anything negative. So we stopped the jeep by the river. We all took off our clothes and dashed into the river and cooled off. It was great. Standing maybe thirty or forty feet away were several Vietnamese women. I think if they'd been American women we would not have just thrown our clothes off and rushed into the water. But they were Vietnamese; they didn't matter; they weren't human for us. So it's interesting to have that transition in Genesis that made clothing a sign of respect in humanity, and that was something our encounters with women in Vietnam very clearly disregarded.

Linda: I knew a fellow in a previous lifetime. I was dating a fellow who was a former marine, and he had been wounded. And he said his perception of women, and the way he viewed them, drastically changed when he was wounded, and wound up in a hospital surrounded by nurses. At that point he had the greatest admiration and respect. Prior to that he didn't. He said that was the turning point for him.

David: Probably wouldn't be fair to not say that my experience of Vietnamese women was different because – again because of the assignment that I had – we had them working for us and I knew them personally by name. And I found myself in the position of having to protect them a few times. So my thoughts about them are different. Including one time when I was appointed on orders as investigating officer for someone who had been fired from working at a PX at another place. You didn't appoint someone from your own place. I went to find out. So she was accused of working with someone to steal U.S. stuff from the PX and it was all the usual "pacing off the distance" kinds of accusations. But the more I found out, the more I discovered that the investigator up there – an Air Force investigator - every sign pointed to him and his girlfriend as being the perpetrators of the very thing depicted. They were throwing blame on her. And when I got close enough to actually find out more, he said you're not at liberty to examine that information because he was intelligence – supposedly. So I put all this in my report, and I told my commander that I think the person should be transferred and re-instated because I think she's getting the shaft big time. He, in fact, decided that's what he would do. I wasn't real popular on that base again after that. But, you know, somewhere in school they told me that "the constitution follows the flag," and I couldn't get rid of that phrase as I was doing this. You can't just do that to her because she Vietnamese and you don't want to get caught for what you're up to.

Phil: The other thing that comes to mind, that strikes me, Jack, as you were saying, about the clothing and how it provides the dignity and respect for the women. You know, every time we were on stand down and we went to he enlisted men's club and it was entertainment, it always ended with a strip show. Whether or not I was conscious to see at the end – most of the time I wasn't – I'd have a designated non-drinker to take pictures so I'd have souvenirs. But it always ended that way. That's another example of how the women were utilized as objects of entertainment. It's very degrading when you look back, but it was entertainment to us; it was helping to get our minds off the next day when we would be going back into the field again on another mission, another ambush, another search and destroy mission. We needed that relief. It was always connected with booze and sex.

Jack: How much difference was there between the women in the strip shows and the "donut dollies?" In terms of women seen and used for entertainment? Here am I out at this forward firebase; and, all of a sudden, a helicopter comes in and off gets a "donut dolly" in a nice crisp uniform, dress, and everything, and she works up a game of volleyball with the guys. I'm still trying to figure that out.

Charlie: What the hell kind of unit was that? I want to join that.

Jack: Didn't happen very often.

Phil: They wore mini-skirts, didn't they?

Linda: That was the style. I have pictures.

John: And what about other kinds of recreation? The "adult dollies" who came around, so we were told, and were "servicing" the officers and sending an awful lot of money home as the result.

Linda: Oh boy.

Jack: I'd want to hear from an officer that that was, in fact, the case.

Ken: It just occurred to me. When I said something earlier about not being able to trust them. When you're out in the field, when you move into a ville, you saw a different Vietnamese woman. You saw the mothers and the grandmothers who sheltered their kids and looked out at you – fearfully. Sometimes they would give rice. I'm just thinking that we need to separate the two pictures here --the one that we see back at the stand-downs in the cities from the one down in the villes.

Ray: That, and those we saw - to expand a bit on what Charlie's said - the first time in the shower when the Vietnamese woman walked in and started to giggle; she was always the one who had the beetle-nut stained teeth...

Charlie: She had black feet too.

Ray: As opposed to the ones in the strip club who were primped and primed.

John: I still can't get over the shower. But the thing that's running around in my head, and I can't really relate it to Eden but I'm going to bring it up anyway, and that's the suspension of conscience that I think we were asked to make or demanded of us. Not only with women, but right across the board. It wasn't drummed into me but I guess I grew up with the golden rule and "thou shalt not kill." I wasn't particularly religious then, but it was instilled in me somehow, and then I went over there and it was like none of that applied. "There's a whole different set rules here and you better get used to it."

Linda: Yes, the morality was totally different. The assumption that I heard about women whoring. I've heard that story handed down before. I do know rumors were floating all over the place. I also know that the first time I went to a VA hospital – let me re-phrase that – the first and only time I have ever been in a VA hospital. I needed to check out something; I wasn't sure if I had malaria or what – The Doctor there picked up my records and looked at them. "Just back from Vietnam, Huh?" I said, "Yeah." And he said, "Did you make a lot of money?" I said, "Well, with proficiency pay and hazardous duty pay, and no place to spend it, I did alright." And he said, "Nah, no, I mean whoring around." That was, of course, when I walked out. There was an assumption that - among some - that women who would go into that situation were there for one reason. And I know we're not supposed to get into any deep personal sharing, but I got a couple comments here. Most people at this table know that I was gang-raped in Vietnam. Two things about that. One was the officer over the men when I reported this to my commander. My commander came back to me and said that he said he would back his men, that it was my party, and that anything happened to me was my own fault because what did women expect by being there in the first place. And then the second thing was – in the process of that they took all my underwear; they took all my clothes – the most personal part of my clothing they took. So much for respect.

Russ: I would like to speak to the point that you brought up earlier about women being expected to be nurturers. And then I heard something about women being in second place?

Linda: Well, you put your own feelings second. You take care of this person first, and you don't worry about how you're feeling about something.

Russ: O.K., but the point is we're all, as ministers, in a nurturing role and does that give us, or does that require us to take, second place? Or does it presume or quickly assume that we are in second place because we are nurturers? That's a toughie, but I think if we're going to talk about gender issues we need to talk about nurture and what does that have to do with how we see ourselves, in the way that nurture is defined?

Linda: That's a valid point. When you go and talk to somebody who just lost somebody, don't they kind of expect – I mean – if you lost somebody, they'd expect you'd know what to do and they wouldn't need to be present to you.

Jack: So you got all this stuff handled?

Linda: Right. Nobody has to take care of him because he knows what to do, so here we are. Sometimes loaded with hurt and where do you take it? That's why you created this organization.

John: And we certainly have heard a lot here how the church, with a capital C, does not take very good care of its people who are wounded. In general, not every time.

Jack: And that it doesn't always take very good care of its ministers.

John: That's what I mean.

Russ: Ministers who may not have been traumatized by war.

John: True.

Alan: So here we are. We put aside the knowledge of good and evil because once you eat of the tree of good and evil, you're going to die. And, as John has said, in order to survive in Vietnam we had to really suspend our knowledge of what we understood to be good and evil and just sort of "do" in order to survive. Of course, we've been talking about the creation story with Adam and Eve, both, according to the Genesis story, sort of miraculously born. But now turn your attention for a minute to the story of the first two human beings, the brothers Cain and Abel. As you read that particular story of Cain and Abel, and as you read it with a veteran's eyes, are there any phrases that strike you?

David: "If you do well, will you not be accepted?" We'd been told if you really try hard enough, you'll be able to accomplish the feat.

John: "Am I my bother's keeper?" Watch out for my fellow soldiers.

Alan: How about "Let us go out into the field."

Jack: That's sergeant talk.

Charlie: Let's not and say we did; "search and avoid."

John: How about "my punishment is greater than I can bear."

Linda: That's in your face. Some people found God in Vietnam; some people lost God in Vietnam.

Phil: One thing that strikes me about this and I've never really thought of it this way before - it has nothing to do with a phrase - but it's the whole story itself. Traditionally in the Jewish Scriptures, the first-born was always the favored offering, the first born sheep, the unblemished, the first born son was the one that was going to inherit everything. And this is the first episode in Scripture where the first-born is not the accepted one. We know later on about Jacob and Esau. But this is the first account when the first-born is rejected, and it's the second child, the young one, it's his gift that's accepted. So it's almost like there's a contradiction there.

Jack: Well, this story is very intriguing from the perspective of the acceptance because if you just stick with this passage, there is no explanation given as to why Cain's offering is not accepted. Now if you look into the New Testament where Paul talks about it, refers back and so forth, then you get this popular notion that Abel had a good offering and Cain had a bad offering and that's why Abel was accepted and Cain wasn't. But if you just stick to this story, if you don't bring in the New Testament, it was just one of those things, probably a Presbyterian pre-ordained kind of thing; Abel's [offering] was ordained to be taken and Cain's was not. And God is kind of surprised that Cain is upset by this.

Bruce: Well, I just view it. . . it says right here what it is – let me read it. "Cain brought to the Lord an offering." Then drop down to Abel . . .

Jack: O.K.

Bruce: So it's like the first fruits; it's like Abel went out and gave God the first of everything he had. Cain just went out and got an offering of whatever he was growing, a nonchalant, self-seeking offering.

Ray: What he gleaned from the field after the pickings.

John: Is this a fundamentalist defending a Presbyterian?

Linda: The fruits of the ground. If you have fruit trees, the fruit that hits the ground is not the best stuff. You go up and pick it. So the fruit on the ground, you just pickup and say, "Here!"

Phil: It says of the ground, not on the ground.

David: We probably have to look at the propaganda value of the story, which I'm sure it was used later that way. Remember that the Israelites coming into Canaan were supposedly pastoralists, sheepherders. The Canaanites were fixed plot farmers raising crops from the ground, so which one did the Lord favor? The ones with the sheep, of course! Our guys! So there's a propaganda value here.

Alan: So the one who's blessed is the one who brings in the animals. It's interesting that Abel brought an offering that was a "blood offering." And that Cain, whose offering was rejected, then brought a "blood offering" by killing his brother,

Linda: No kidding.

Alan: But he was reluctant to admit it.

David: There's another line in here that occurs to me, goes back to the question you first asked, "Anyone who meets me may kill me." You never knew who might be the one who was going to kill you.

Alan: "I shall be a fugitive and a wanderer; anyone who meets me may kill me."

David: Just casually one day, next to that Vietnamese induction center across the road from our compound, there was a little card shop where, when they actually got time away, they went in there. Apparently somebody felt he was cheated one day and he happened to be VC. So he threw a satchel charge in there and tossed one over the fence to us for good measure. You never know when it's going to happen. Anyone who meets me can kill me.

Charlie: There's a good guilt phrase here for us. "What have you done? Your brother's blood cries out from the ground."

Alan: What about that phrase?

Charlie: It happens after dark, between dark and sun-up, that portion of the day.

Alan: "Your brother's blood cries out from the ground." That resonate with anybody?

John: What about the anguish that a lot of us feel about people that were lost, that died, that we couldn't save, should have saved, should have been there.

Phil: Or people we killed by accident.

Bruce: Maybe even the Wall in DC is the blood of our brothers crying out from the ground.

Charlie: I always think of the kid's head we split with a shell flare; that one's always stuck in my head. We had to do it because we were going under, so we opened up. The village was in our splash area. There were lots of rounds that went wide of the margin. The kid is definitely …. Maybe all those other people who were hurt. It was really bad day. Mother's Day – 12th of May, 1969.

Ken: Also, I think somebody was talking about when he came home; he got spit at, or slugged at an airport.

David: I got a *sig heil* salute.

Ken: There we go. We've heard the others. That we had been charged with being bloody killers and we never thought we were. We thought we'd come back to Eden – what was it, the land of the big PX – "Back to the world?"

Alan: "Back to the world."

Ken: Yeah. "Back to the world."

Charlie: The "real world."

Ken: The "real world" and everything would be all right there, no matter what we did.

Bruce: We were surprised that we were blamed for fighting the war – for the war itself.

Ken: We lost our innocence in the sense that we went over there with a sense of purpose to try and do some good. We came back thinking maybe we had done some good, and we were castigated.

Jack: One of the reasons that I put forth my interpretation on the Cain and Abel thing, and I can certainly see how you can get, in fact, say Abel's offering was acceptable and Cain's was defective in some fashion. But there's some power in seeing it the other way, and in the other way it resonates with the Vietnam experience. Because in a sense, I mean certainly any of us who went over as volunteers, but really anybody who even was willing to be drafted, as opposed to really taking the other direction and going to Canada or Sweden or something, really was making an offering of themselves and of their lives to their country and at the end of the year you come back and realize that *that* offering is not accepted. O.K. So in the analogy, Cain is replaced by us, God is replaced by the country, but the feeling is still there. Maybe it wasn't the best; maybe it was defective; but still it was our offering and we gave it and we come back. And we get *sig heil* salutes; we get spit in the face; we get the kind of reaction that we did and . . .

Linda: And we are banned from Eden; we are banned from our homeland.

Bruce: And we have the mark of Cain. Do we have that mark?

Charlie: I felt like dirt. I was in the shower and it didn't matter.

Russ: This is a passage that suggests some are winners and some are losers, and that's just the way it is.

Charlie: I don't think we're losers.

Russ: This cannot be a win-win.

Charlie: Don't even go there, Russ. You're about to step off into a deep shit-hole right there.

Alan: Charlie, how do you really feel about that?

Bruce: Somehow maybe the whole Bible is about winning and losing; the whole set up from the time Satan becomes the adversary of God, the whole story is winning and losing.

Russ: How can we be in a win-win situation? It may really tell the human condition.

Ray: I think that – and I know again Linda said we're not supposed to go into deep personal sharing – however . . .

Charlie: Just the deep!

Ray: After spending two months in the hospital – Tripler Army Hospital in Hawaii - based on injuries that I had received and a fungus that had grown henceforth, calling my commanding officer to request pay records, and being told that I was listed as a deserter because they had no record of my having been hospitalized. They then received them, but when I returned I felt like Cain because all the rest of the guys that I had been with for the year treated me as if I, in fact, had deserted and they were just bringing me back for my punishment, and that. . . And the other piece of that is I had a taste of – I won't say Eden – but I certainly would say the good life during that two months because I was back in the "real world" and then to be sent back after sixty-three days of "real world" to. . . With all of that shit going on, it certainly made you feel like you had the mark of Cain upon you.

Alan: What is the mark of Cain? If we bear it?

Ray: What was the scarlet letter?

Jack: You know in the Biblical version the mark of Cain is

a protection; it's a mercy given to Cain so that he would not be subject to being killed and beaten up and *seig heil*'ed by everybody that wanted to.

Ken: But he can never go home.

Phil: He's an aimless wanderer.

John: In the land of Nod, in the east.

Bruce: And maybe the stigma of Vietnam vets – "you know, you've got to watch out for these guys." That stigma may have protected us from beatings and everything else because people were afraid of us. For the first decade after the war people were absolutely afraid to hire a veteran, because they were afraid he was going to go crazy or whatever. But maybe that was the mark that was God's protection of us. Let people thing that we would do them in if they talked bad towards us.

John: Weren't the "spin numbers" the mark of Cain?

Jack: The which numbers?

John: The "spin numbers."

Alan: The "spin numbers" on your service record.

Phil: The lottery, or what?

John: On your 214 there's a code number that everybody got and if you were pushed out of the military for some reason they didn't like, such as being gay, or "unsuitable" was another, or hard to get along with, there was a certain code. All the employers were given the code sheets.

Phil: I didn't know that.

Ken: Is that right?

Alan: Yup.

Phil: I'll have to look at my DD214. Where's the code at?

Ken: Can we get a copy of the code?

Phil: Look at Ray; he's got a 214 on him!

Linda: I've got mine; I always carry mine.

Ken: We're talking about the code though.

Linda: Oh, you mean the code.

Ray: The "spin numbers" are on the bottom of the top right hand corner.

Bruce: How do you decipher it though?

Ken: That's what we need to know.

John: I've got a code sheet I can send you.

Bruce: I'd like to have that.

Charlie: Make one for me.

Bruce: After spending seven years in Canada; they may have something weird going on with mine.

John: What's amazing is these were given out to all these employers and seems like most veterans never even knew about it.

Russ: Well, I just found out about it.

David: I sure never knew about it.

Phil: You knew about it because you worked in the system.

Bruce: I did the freedom of information act because two years of my records have been stripped, the last two years. And that's when I was involved with [other stuff], so I did a freedom of information thing trying to figure out what was going on with my records, and of course, they don't – I've got letters at home – we don't know you, we've never heard of you, and on and on and on and on. They sent a guy to Canada to check on me. That'll be interesting to see what the "spin number" is.

Jack: Yeah. I'm trying to go back now. It seems like this "we don't know who you are" is such a profound statement it's got to appear in one of the Biblical stories somewhere but I can't place it.

Linda: Well, Jesus, in the Gospel, said it, you come to the gate of heaven, "I don't know who you are."

Ken: In the parable.

Jack: In Matthew 25. I never knew you. Right.

Linda: Yeah. Right.

John: "We don't know who you are" could be to you.

Jack: But, Bruce, there's also Peter at the temple while Jesus is off being questioned.

Alan: I want to get back to this question of blood, and the sacrifice that is offered by Abel that is acceptable is a blood offering, the first of the flock. Then Cain offers up the first-born, his brother, by killing him. Does this possibly give us a paradigm for what was expected of us? Did God and country, interchangeable in many ways, demand a blood offering? And did we make it?

John: 58,000 of them.

Charlie: That's just what I say.

Ken: The blood offering – we're thirty years later – still bleeding.

Alan: Who's bleeding now?

Ken: We are.

John: Blood, sweat, and tears.

Called to Service

Excerpts from Genesis 12 and 13 (NRSV)

Now the Lord said to Abram, "Go from your country and your kindred and your father's house to the land that I will show you. I will make of you a great nation, and I will bless you, and make your name great, so that you will be a blessing . . ."

So Abram went, as the Lord had told him; and Lot went with him . . . Abram took his wife Sarai and his brother's son Lot, and all the possessions that they had gathered . . . and they set forth to go to the land of Canaan . . . Then the Lord appeared to Abram, and said, "To your offspring I will give this land." So he built there an altar to the Lord, who had appeared to him . . . And Abram journeyed on by stages toward the Negeb.

Now there was a famine in the Land. So Abram went down to Egypt to reside there . . . When he was about to enter Egypt, he said to his wife Sarai, "I know well that you are a woman beautiful in appearance; and when the Egyptians see you, they will say, 'This is his wife'; then they will kill me, but they will let you live. Say you are my sister, so that it may go well with me because of you, and that my life may be spared on your account . . ." The Egyptians saw that the woman was very beautiful. When the officials of Pharaoh saw her, they praised her to Pharaoh. And the woman was taken into Pharaoh's house. And for her sake he dealt well with Abram; and he had sheep, oxen, male donkeys, male and female slaves, female donkeys, and camels.

Bu the Lord afflicted Pharaoh and his house with great plagues because of Sarai, Abram's wife. So Pharaoh called Abram, and said, "What is this you have done to me? Why did you not tell me that she was your wife? Why did you say, 'She is my sister,' so I took her for my wife? Now then, here is your wife; take her, and be gone." And Pharaoh gave his men orders concerning him; and they set him on the way, with his wife and all that he had.

So Abram went up from Egypt, he and his wife, and all that he had, and Lot with him, into the Negeb. As far as Beth-el, to the place where his tent had been at the beginning, between Beth-el and Ai, to the place where he had made an altar at the first; and there Abram called on the name of the Lord.

* * * * *

Participating: Alan, Charlie, Bruce, David, Ray, Jack, John, Ken, Linda, Phil, Russ

* * * * *

Alan: "Go from your country and your kindred and your father's house to the land I will show you. I will make of you a great nation, and I will bless you, and make your name great so that you will be a blessing." This is the part of Genesis called the "call to Abram" or Abraham. He's called forth with a promise of great blessing. Now when you were called to service for your nation, did you consider it a call of great blessing? Did you perhaps volunteer? How did you get there?

Russ: I was about to starve. I had to get some money. So I went and got commissioned.

Bruce: Well, that was in 1919.

John: We're talking about the Vietnam War.

Russ: My motivation was less than divine.

Phil: I was a draftee. I got this letter, but I knew exactly what it was without opening it. But I knew it was coming. I was working and I'd left school so I knew they would eventually find me. But I was not going to volunteer. I was drafted, and, first reaction, it was not a blessing. I don't know if I considered it a curse, but it certainly was something I was very afraid of. Because it'd be my first time away from home, and not knowing exactly what I'd be going into, so it was frightening.

Alan: I can remember the first time I was summoned for a physical by my local draft board. I was working on my master's degree and I got this notice to show up for a physical – from the Selective Service – to go into Boston. And so I showed up, 5:30 in the morning, got on this bus with a bunch of other guys, and we went in. I took the physical and when the results came out, I was classified 1-Y, because I had a heart condition. So I said to my parents, "Hey, I'm 1-Y." And they said, "What's does that mean?" "It means I won't be called unless there's some sort of emergency because I've got some sort of a medical problem." I thought everything was hunky-dory, and I just went on making plans to go back to school, to do what I was doing. The next month I got another summons to go back to Boston for a physical. So I went back to Boston for a second time, went through the whole thing, came out 1-Y. I said, "O.K., I guess they just want to make sure I wasn't kidding around." Well, the third month it happened I began to wonder, but I went in for a third time and came up 1-Y again. The fourth month – I don't know whether the doctor was deaf or had an ear infection – but I went through the whole thing, I got to the doctor, he listened to my heart, said everything was fine. They pulled me out and said, "You don't need to take the rest. You're 1-A now."

Linda: Duh!

Alan: And so I just sort of sat there and I waited. In due course a letter came saying "Your friends and neighbors have selected you . . . ." It gave me a date to show up, and I pulled a few strings because I knew the Selective Service law. Well, since they couldn't draft me out of a semester in which I was currently enrolled, I enrolled in a year's worth of semesters ahead of time, and then I went down and told them "You can't draft me. I'm currently enrolled in a semester next year." They were really kind of upset with me for that. They were going to get me and I needed an extra four months to finish my master's degree, so I went to the navy; and the day before I was being drafted I enlisted in the navy under a four month delay so I could finish my master's degree. But it certainly wasn't what you would consider a blessing that somehow my name was mud with my Selective Service board because I gave them such a hard time. And I don't remember anything very blessed about the four physicals, you know, standing around with 200 other young men in your underwear for four hours.

John: I'd think three out of four would be enough.

Alan: Yeah, You'd think so.

Ken: Well, I had a much different experience. I had been ordained a year or two, I guess, and I got a phone call from the recruiting chaplain for the First Army Area looking for reserve chaplains. He had the name of a priest at the diocese who had been in the army and had evidenced some interest in going back in as a chaplain. He couldn't find him in the roster so he found our parish number and he called asking, "Where is this guy?" So I gave him the guy's address and number and that was the last I heard of it. Two days later this guy called me back and said, "He said, 'No.' How about you?" We had a reserve unit in the parish

– physically located in the parish – they used to come to Mass on Sundays in a two-ton – whatever those big trucks were – anyway a big truck with those guys lined up in the back. The pastor was really very affected by their presence; he thought it was a good thing. And when this other guy called, he said, "Sure. Go ahead." So I ended up in the reserves. About a year later I get a notice that the archbishop wants to talk with me; it seems he'd gotten a letter from somebody in Washington telling him that I was a very effective young chaplain and would he please release me to go on active duty? The archbishop wanted to know with whom I had arranged this, so I could get out of the diocese and into the army. But it had been a computer-generated letter to every bishop and superior in the country who had a company grade – I was a second lieutenant -- reserve officer or National Guard. They were so desperate at that point.

Jack: So every single chaplain on the list was exceptionally qualified?

Ken: Yes. And I happened to be the only one in the diocese. There were a couple colonels and such – a little *supra adulta* – but anyway, when I went down to talk to the archbishop and he was quite open to this whole thing. He said, "You can do it, or you don't have to." But his nephew had been killed in Nam about three months earlier and the family had been very much consoled and touched by some army chaplain who had come to the house and been at the funeral and the whole bit. He said, "They're really needed. If you want to do it, it's O.K. by me. There are no strings attached. You don't have to." And forty-five minutes later I walked out of his office with a release, and six weeks later I was in the army. That's how I ended up in the army. Totally accidental all the way along the line. It's like – you know – you move here – you move there – you move back there. That's what happened. Crazy. Seven years later I got out.

John: I can remember thinking it was a duty and an honor. It's really amazing to me now. I grew up in a place in northern New Hampshire where it was just the expected thing. My father had all the photographs on the wall of soldiers. He never said anything about it, but the pictures said to me, "War is hell, but necessary." There wasn't any blood-n-guts in the pictures; just a bunch of men standing around – they weren't smiling – but there was this gorgeous woman in the picture with them in France. I said, "Oh, that's the way it must be."

Phil: Nice day, eh?

Jack: You joined up for the women, didn't you?

John: Travel and adventure!

Ken: France was the other woman.

John: What did I know?

David: But they used to have Vietnam . . . so close, right!

Jack: The duty thing certainly was there, both as part of the official ideology of the draft and everything else, but also matched by the feelings of a lot of us. My own experience really started out when I went into college. I'd never given any thought to the military before and I discovered the college had compulsory ROTC. I did the freshman year, but struggled with it the whole time in terms of my Christian beliefs about war and everything else. Over that summer I wrote a piece to the president of the college asking for exemption as a conscientious objector. And I was granted that status. Unfortunately you just can't take thinking and turn it on and then turn it off when it's done. So I kept thinking through the thing during that semester I was exempted as a conscientious objector, and finally figured out that no, I couldn't be a pure conscientious objector. There were situations under which I could take another life and, given that, it didn't feel like it was right to continue that status. So I became the only male at Western Maryland campus to take ROTC voluntarily. I went back, made up the missing time, went advanced, got a commission out of the thing, so all the time that I was at seminary it was just assumed I was going to go on active duty, and by the time I went on active duty it was assumed that, if you were on active duty, you were going to Vietnam. So that was my parallel to the Abraham thing.

Ray: When I was at school at a Presbyterian College down south – I was raised a good Presbyterian, then I saw the light - but anyway - I realized I was just wasting my time. It was my first time away from home. I had earned over the summer $1500; and, before going to school, spent it all on booze and clothes and thought, "This was quite the waste." And that, even though I felt called to ministry, I ought to grow up before I accepted that call. On my English final, I wrote a letter to the professor - Dr. B****, who at the beginning of the semester hated my guts because I was the quote-unquote "only goddamned Yankee" in his class – and for the final exam I wrote this letter explaining my reasons why I, number one, wasn't taking the final exam and, number two, why I was leaving the school. He was in the teacher's lounge and I took the letter down to him. He said, "Ray, have a seat." I thought, "Oh shit!" It wasn't something that I really relished doing. His remarks after reading the letter were basically, "I wish that more people could be like you because there are too many people here who should not be here yet are here because they do not have the drive, the desire, to be what you feel called to be." When I arrived home bag and baggage my folks asked me what I was going to do now. I said I had already had done it. Well, I'd enlisted in the army – with the promise of going to OCS and the whole business, so that's why I was a "RA" *["Regular Army" or*

"RA" was a designation to indicate someone who was a career person, rather then a "US" which was used to designate people with a limited term of enlistment or commission] instead of a "US" which was always – in boot camp – it was always, "Oh, you're one of those "RA's," huh? You must really suck this stuff up." Which was not necessarily the case, but I did feel a sense of call to duty. Besides that my draft number was seventeen, so I was dead meat anyway.

Alan: There was a sense, that I can remember, that going into the service, though I sort of wiggled about a bit before I got there, that this was going to put me in the same league with my uncle who had been in World War Two – and who'd always been a lot of fun to be around. I never thought much about it later, but looking back on it I can see that he never talked about anything that happened to him as a bombardier in the Pacific. But I thought that by joining the armed forces I would be part of that great heritage of the World War Two soldier - of course, no one talked about Korea – never heard anything about that – it was still all about World War Two. We went into the military in different ways with different kinds of experiences. What about when you got orders to Vietnam? How did you react to that particular call? Did you expect it?

David: I've got to tell both things since you put it that way. I've never quite understood why, but when I was in high school I thought, "I ought to go to West Point." I actually got a letter from my congressman saying, "O.K., you're appointed as a second alternate." I went to take the physical at the Presidio of San Francisco, stayed two days in the barracks there. I'd gone out for baseball in high school about three weeks before – and I'd pulled a muscle right down here. And you know, seven of the eight physical aptitude tests involved running or jumping, and I flunked it completely. I said, "I don't want to wait another year; I'll take ROTC instead." So I went to junior college for two years, but took ROTC at Berkeley – you know how it was – the same idea – you've got to be part of this tradition. My family had - when they could – had been part of whatever needed to be done. They just didn't say "no" when there was a duty to be performed of some kind. I continued that until I graduated from UC Berkeley and I knew from right about the middle of the time in ROTC that I was going to Vietnam – they had told me so. So the day I went on active duty, my active duty orders said your assignment to Vietnam will be around October of 1970 and I said, "Oh, I knew that." That was my reaction. I don't know why it wasn't anything else because I sure had been watching the news and I had seen guys that had come back, and still it was just kind of an empty reaction. Maybe it was a denial or something, but there wasn't much reaction to speak of except that, "I already knew that."

Alan: Sort of resignation.

David: You might call it that. That would be a fair description.

Linda: I pulled strings to go. I mean I literally worked all the angles so I could get there, naively believing that it was going to be something different than it was. Naively believing that as a woman I would be safe, not in any kind of danger. And looked upon it, naively, as a great adventure and exciting. That lasted about twenty minutes in country because when we landed at Bien Hoa, the Bien Hoa airport came under attack. The . . . As I was laying on the ground I thought. "This may have been a mistake."

David: Yeah. Or something close to that.

Linda: I really believed it was the right thing to do. I believed we were right in being there, in the evil empire of the communists . . . I bought the whole thing until I was part of it.

Phil: And then it was too late.

Linda: At that point I was already sucked into the whirlpool and there was no way out. I just had to go with it, and I've thought less of myself ever since.

Phil: I remember when I got my orders to Nam. There wasn't any surprise because I was infantry. Basically I had AIT in infantry – my MOS – I knew I was going to go. I remember getting those orders at Fort Ord giving us two weeks furlough to go home and have a little break before we went. I don't remember if I called my folks up on the phone or waited till I got home to tell them. But I remember those two weeks; it was tense at home – being an only child and all that – and I knew that I wanted not to disgrace my family because my father was a World War Two veteran - served honorably – so there was no way I wanted to do anything that would bring shame to him, although I was really scared. They threw me a big going away party and all the friends – my high school friends and everyone came over and we had dancing and drinking – a lot of drinking -- it was really a lot of fun. One thing I remember – just remembered now for the first time – it was the night before I left – the party was; and I remember my mother didn't sleep that night, and all of a sudden I heard a commotion from the next room where my mother and father were sleeping – she had had too much to drink – my mother never over-drank – and she had become hysterical and she was laughing, crying, and having uncontrollable diarrhea at the same time. And she had messed her bed. I had never seen her naked – she didn't remember anything the next morning – I remember my father holding her on the toilet seat, trying to keep her down because she was throwing up, and defecating at the same time, but laughing, giggling like a child. I had never seen my mother naked before. I got up and I was saying, "My God, what's going on with her?" I was so scared I thought she was dying or something. And I remember my dad slapping her in the face, trying to bring her to her senses – trying to bring her back – the more he slapped her the more she laughed. I never remembered that story and I don't know why it comes up now. But it's all got to do with leaving. Then later on my dad – when I did come back – told me that right after the March 1st incident when I told them what had happened – she had nearly had a nervous breakdown and he almost had to put her in the hospital. So all of that stuff is kind of really weird – bringing all that back. I know we're not supposed to do personal sharing, but this is kind of something that was part of that whole feeling of – it was a going away party; it was fun! Yet I was going into a place where I, at that point, I thought, "I'll be back." I was very optimistic. I never . . . . I didn't expect . . . until I got there . . . what was going to happen. I think I was still under the impression that it was "John Wayne," that it was "guns and glory." But I had no intentions of not coming back.

John: I had such a feeling of foreboding that I wouldn't be back

Linda: I can remember my mother saying, when they dropped me off at the airport, at that moment she was standing there – and she was in tears – and I said, "Mom, I'll be all right." And she said, "I'm not crying for you. I'm just glad it's you and not your brothers." And she meant that not in a negative way towards me, but she was looking around and here were all these young men in fatigues and ready to go. And I got on the plane and she knew some of them wouldn't come back. And she said that was when she changed her mind about whether of not it was a proper war.

Jack: Whether or not what?

Linda: Whether or not it was a proper war.

Ken: You know Abraham is portrayed in tradition as the just, faithful, obedient man. I wonder how happy he was to be picked up form the land of Ur – do I have that right? Ur of the Chaldeans. To be picked up, told to go some place else, then to be replanted in Egypt, and then get replanted back. They leave it out. "What are you doing to me?"

John: Another thing I wonder; I wonder if God spoke to Creighton Abrams.

Charlie: And was he listening?

John: Apparently not.

Alan: "And bless you and make your name great so that you will be a great blessing." That phrase about being a great blessing comes up again and again. I didn't know if I was going to be great or anything. But I remember the day that I'd made it through OCS and all the orders came in. Everybody kind of got them in a bunch – some people were going to destroyer school, somebody else was assigned to a minesweeper, guys were going to supply school, and everybody got their orders but me. I got a message that the C. O. wanted to see me down in his office. I went down and he put me at "parade rest" and told me that he wanted to give me my orders personally because he was so "damn proud." Out of the entire class that graduated with me at OCS I was the only one that got orders directly to Vietnam, because I spoke North Vietnamese. And I can remember standing in his office at parade rest as he was telling me how proud he was, and the only thing that I could think of was, "Oh shit! I'm dead." You know, I had that kind of foreboding that I would not be coming back.

Linda: But we were right. We didn't come back. We came back as somebody else.

Alan: That's a good point about Abraham having been drafted and moved from place to place to place. It doesn't tell us how he reacted to it really. It just says that there is this promise that goes before him. He goes to the land of Canaan – which was inhabited, of course, by the Canaanites – but the Lord was going to let him "occupy" it; so Abraham's call was to go out and "occupy" somebody else's land. Did you feel – I know I felt a little bit like an occupying force when I was shoved around. We'd taken the prime waterfront up in Danang and turned it into military installations and chased all the locals out, and wouldn't let them come back in unless they checked back in and worked for us as hooch maids, or whatever they were hired as.

John: The "Americanization."

Alan: Yeah.

Jack: You notice . . . I was very clear in my own mind as I drove my jeep from Plieku to An Khe on Route 19 – which by that point the engineers had built up probably a foot and a half with macadam – there was no way anyone could stick a mine in that! It was so thick, and it was nice; it was a smooth blacktop road, better than anything you find stateside. On the side of the road – I've got a picture on my internet site – a picture I took – a nice white sign with a nice red, white, and blue interstate-type shield with a "19E" there and then a slogan "Highway 19, paved for your driving comfort by the such and such army engineers." It was very clear to me at that point that as long as we simply could go about taking over their country and do it our way, things were going to be fine So that fits right into Abraham going into Canaan. Of course, there were just a couple of Canaanites in Vietnam that took umbrage at that.

Charlie: More than a couple. They drove their T-55 tanks down that road real well, and we finished it all the way out to the border so they didn't have to get too muddy! I always wondered why they let us build those bridges; they drove tanks over them; finally we figured out why.

Alan: We've got Abraham and his blessing and he goes off to occupy the land. There's a famine and he goes off to another place; he goes off to Egypt. He's not having a very easy time of . .

Charlie: Or Cambodia, which one was it?

Alan: No, no. Egypt, not Cambodia.

Charlie: First he went to Vietnam; then he went to Cambodia.

Alan: Or something like that. He goes down with his wife, and if you read this particular passage you find – both at the beginning and the end – Abraham is blessed. You know he gets the blessing that he is going to occupy the land of Canaan – at the end of the thing he's gotten rich in livestock and silver and gold so he had all kinds of things; but in between this, you've got this strange little story of him going down to Egypt and saying to his wife Sarai, "Act like you're my sister, not my wife."

Linda: "And the story is . . ."

Alan: Yeah. "The story is . . ."

Jack: So it was a brief incursion into a neighboring country characterized by dishonesty!

David: The secret war in Laos, is that the one you're talking about?

Alan: The one in Cambodia.

Ken: Actually it was to save his own skin that she was to

pass off as his sister.

David: That's what it says there, but read the rest of it too. He ends up real rich out of this and he tries the same scam another time. Remember?

Ken: He was operating Air America.

David: The next time the story appears, he does it again!

Linda: And probably still the same scam.

David: Something like – but I wonder if he had thoughts ahead of time about working this number on Pharaoh.

Bruce: Well, Isaac did the same thing to the same guy that his dad did it to. Abimalech.

Jack: Really?

Bruce: You go a bit further and you'll see that Abraham's son Isaac said the same thing to Rebekah. "Lie – you're my sister."

Jack: Boy, these foreigners are sure stupid, aren't they?

Bruce: Well, Abimalech fell for it again.

Alan: Hey, if you're going to survive you'll do what you've got to do.

Jack: Again and again.

John: That's why he moved around a lot.

Alan: Couldn't stay in one place.

Ray: As an air cav unit we moved about wherever we were called to go. We started out at Dian. And from there we went to Lai Khe, then Phuc Bien, back to Lai Khe, back to Dian, and then down to Vinh Long. And that was, like, every time we turned around. We questioned whether or not we should even unpack the Conex containers because we knew we would be moving.

Alan: You know, I hadn't thought about that – until you were just saying it – but even when I was in country it seemed that I was never really stationed just in one place for that long a time. It was very much "We need you to go there" or "We need you to go here." Just kept moving. Eventually, I can remember, I had luggage in three different places in Vietnam.

Ken: And it's still there.

Alan: As far as I know, some of it still is!

Charlie: You have to wonder what the Viet Cong did with those old sermons that I left.

Russ. "Slicky boys" stole my briefcase that had sermons in it; and I hated that terribly.

John: What did you call them? "Slicky boys?"

David: "Slicky boys."

Russ: "Slicky boys."

Bruce: "Slicky boys and boom-boom girls."

David: You don't know the verb form "to slicky"? "To slicky" your watch?

Charlie: I thought that was a Korean term. I've been in Korea too.

Russ: Well, I've been there. Been both places.

David: But "mama san" isn't Vietnamese either. A lot of stuff got adapted from pidgin Japanese.

Alan: When I was reading some of this all I could think of was "Well, he did pretty well out of the supply system!"

David: Yes. Well, now you're talking my area -- quartermaster!

John: Tiger stripe shirts!

Bruce: It wasn't in my division.

Jack: You probably had a certain attrition of items.

David: Well, I was once told, "Here are 150 air conditioners that you have to send to property disposal." Well, some them made it to property disposal.

Charlie: Air conditioners?

David: After that I never had a problem getting anything accounted for because the property disposal officer signed for everything that I asked him to. Because his whole unit was air-conditioned after that. Abraham? I understand the situation.

Charlie: Did you have air conditioners?

Jack: What was that?

Charlie: Did you have an air conditioner?

Russ: I did.

Jack: No.

Russ: I had one.

David: I never had one myself.

Russ: I had one in my room.

John: I never had anything to air condition!

Phil: We were under the clear blue sky.

Jack: But I was in the central Highlands. We wore coats up there.

Charlie: It wasn't clear and blue in the monsoon.

Phil: Well, it was green – under the cover.

Charlie: I saw an air conditioner once. They had it in the fire direction center because the computer couldn't work without it.

David: I had a call from a guy at an airbase who said, "We have an emergency here today at the PX at X airbase." I said, "What's your emergency?" He said, "Our air conditioning is out in our office." And I said, "I'll get somebody right up there!" And I will send somebody one of these days, but I haven't done it yet. So you had to be in the right service at the right place. They had air conditioners at a lot of places at that air base.

Russ: War is hell.

Charlie: War is hell.

Alan: You talk about the variety of experience. Just taking a simple poll around here about who had air conditioners and who didn't shows how diverse this particular war was. It really depended upon where you were what you had to do to survive, what point in Egypt you were, whether you had to turn your wife into your sister, or whether you had to work the black market, or what kinds of things you had to do.

Charlie: What if you didn't have a wife or sister?

Russ: You needed a cash register.

John: It's a metaphor, Charlie.

Alan: You were shit-outa-luck.

Ken: I like John's comment that some of us didn't have anything to air condition.

David: Right.

Linda: That's true.

Charlie: There's another level of "no house at all." No one knew it all.

Phil: Living in a poncho liner.

Ken: A poncho liner!

Charlie: Hey, don't knock it!

Alan: It was always amazing to me to see how, in a strange land, when I got there in '71, how incredibly comfortable the Americans could makes themselves.

John: Sure.

Alan: I had this vision from television of people slogging through rice paddies and what have you. And then you arrive in Saigon and there are these tremendous clubs; even up in Danang the accommodations were almost actually palatial, better than what I'd had in language school in the United States.

Bruce: Obviously all that footage was taken when I was there.

Alan: I thought I kept seeing you going through the scenes.

Charlie: Like PBS, they show the same footage again,

David: Over and over.

Ray: I think that when during the last part of my time in country – of course, having gone over as a unit so many of us rotated out at the same time. We'd been up to Mui Ba Dinh working that area for some time. We were called literally out of the field saying that, "You've done your twelve; it's time to go home." And, pardon my French, but I'll be a son of a bitch if they didn't hit the base camp and the one thing that they hit was the big – must have been a five hundred gallon - tank of water that provided the showers for everybody. It just so happened that it rained and I wish I had taken a picture of it, except I was in the midst of it. The corrugated tin that was the roof that provided excellent little water spouts; and you just prayed to God that it rained long enough that you could get the damned soap off of you.

Russ: As far as the text is concerned, and as far as the reports and stories that we are gathering together, the deception, the practiced deception – there seems to be no blush about that kind of thing with Abraham. Pharaoh is taken aback that he's got taken in! There seems to be no conscience to the deception that was practiced here, and it's easy to say that was then and this is now, and we are more enlightened but . . .

Ken: Have you read McNamara's book about . . .

Russ: Yes, I have.

Ken: . . . the awareness of the deception.

Alan: Say some more about that, Ken.

Ken: Just that they were aware of the fact that they had screwed up and made a mistake, but they were so committed that they stayed. They continued the stories. They continued sending more guys, putting out news reports that were false. I remember we were in the Delta – this has nothing to with McNamara – we were in a firefight and we were living with the navy on those supply ships that were part of that force. We came in three or four days later filthy, and they'd hose us down on the pontoons - on the barges – and then let you on the ships so you didn't bring any disease in – any fungi – we had the TV on in the wardroom that night and they talked about the battle and gave us the body count. We went "Who? Where?" Just the deception that was practiced.

Russ: McNamara and Abraham - because Abraham was the father of his people – the deception that you talked about at the average level – enlisted, whoever - is one thing; but it didn't matter at which level, the deception was there and it doesn't make any difference. Abraham and his son and wives. Deception was just practiced.

Linda: I think about my work in the communication area, about when I first became aware of the deception was when we were processing troop movements, other reports. We were also processing casualty reports and knew how many messages we were processing a day. There were specific items in there. But then when the "Stars and Stripes" came out, they would give counts that never seemed to match. And I was confused by this. Finally I started checking; I tried to keep count and wait to see what came out in the "Stars and Stripes." For example, there was this one event where a truck – a deuce and a half – was carrying troops was moving up Highway 1, and the driver got shot, sniper fire or whatever, and was killed. The truck rolled off something and everybody on the truck was killed – when it went out over the cliff. According to the "Stars and Stripes" report there was only one person killed there by enemy fire. They didn't even mention the other guys. I thought, "Wait a minute.

Something's wrong."

Bruce: Wonder if they got purple hearts, or just the guy who got killed got one.

Linda: I don't know that. They have to be on the Wall because they died there. But still what was reported was not accurate.

Ken: You said something during the last session about being angry when you came back. Isn't that an emotion we've all had over the years? An anger that we were deceived and maybe we deceived; and we let it happen to us or we didn't? I think maybe that's some of the bleeding or pain we still carry.

John: Maybe it covers up some of the other stuff too. Anger is safer.

Linda: I was going to say "anger is safer."

Ken: Instead of what they made me do.

John: I had no control

Linda: Except that anger in women is not permissible!

Ken: Oh, that's right.

Bruce: Same in clergy.

John: This thing about Pharaoh and kind of seeing him as us – and Abraham and Sarah as the Vietnamese – we liked the way she looked, so we gave them sheep and oxen and all this stuff including slaves – us – to help then out.

Jack: That's a good analysis. I was caught by something else in there, which is, going back to the spiritual side of things, the relationship of God and Abraham. God is very clearly there at the beginning of the story because God sends Abraham. And at that point, I mean Abraham does not go through any psychologizing or decision-making or self-doubts or reflections or any of this stuff. God says "Go," and he goes. So God's very, very totally active at this moment of the story and God basically, as far as this particular page is concerned, disappears; God isn't there to hold Abraham's hand as he goes through this process. There's no record in this story - whoever wrote it didn't think is was important to tell us whether or not Abraham consulted with God periodically or frequently or any of this stuff. It's like God is absent from the rest of the story, even though God is totally present at the beginning of it. And I guess that strikes me in terms of my own experience of going over to Vietnam as a chaplain, that I went there with a clear feeling that this was what God wanted me to do; but it was kind of like when I got there I was on my own. I had to figure it out. I found, actually my father had saved something I sent to him, they put me on AFVN radio for a series of little fifteen minutes or so - a week with the Chaplain sort of . . .

Charlie: You had that? I did that stuff.

Jack: Right. My father had saved it – I sent it to my father – the draft of the thing. He had saved it and I was reading it a year ago . . .

Ken: That's dangerous!

Jack: It is! Gee, I was trying so hard to say something of relevance to anybody. You can see that I was trying to do this. And there was nothing there in terms of my current theology that I would actually disagree with, but it was just like – I was trying so hard to be helpful and it didn't work. It really didn't work.

Bruce: The door was only ten feet away.

Phil: Did all the chaplains do that?

Jack: I don't know. All I knew was I was called down.

Charlie: Yeah. Those guys back in Camp Enari, they weren't in the war. They had duty rosters. Did you do the TV deal?

Jack: What TV deal?

Charlie: You go up to the studio and you tape the message up there on top of Dragon Mountain. You must have been too far out. I can remember I had to go there and record the TV message, and I had only one pair of clean uniforms left. And I spent the night in a ditch. It was my only clean uniform, so I went on the TV. Maybe it didn't get aired.

Jack: Well, I was only at Camp Enari for a time.

Charlie: Well, I wasn't at Camp Enari. I had to hitch hike in a deuce and a half to get there. If you don't show up, you get this RVI [report for visual inspection] note. These guys were out to lunch. The division is out to lunch! They really were.

John: That's a given.

Bruce: That's a given. Right.

Jack: Well, I must have been at Camp Enari for the radio, but most of the time I was in the field.

Linda: Charlie, if you're waiting for an argument on that statement, you'll wait a long time.

Charlie: Well, I got the note, "You must come to Camp Enari" no matter what. I was way, way out there. I had helicopters and trucks and I was covered with dust and I got down there. My face was dust; my clothes were dust; I was dust all over. I go up to the shower. Guy says, "You can't take a shower." I said, "Why not?" "The troops in the field can't take a shower." I said, "What do I look like? Joe-shit, the ragman? I mean, you know, explain this to me because I ain't getting this at all." So I went in all dusty and that's when we got chewed out because some chaplain got his picture in Time magazine carrying a weapon with a bandoleer.

Ken: Oh, yeah,

Charlie: Boy, was I pissed!

Ken: That was M****.

Charlie: Was it M****? I said, "You jerked my chain, you risked my life – I shaved my legs for this! I came all the way in here for this!!" Damn, man, I'm not mad!

John: Blood pressure time!

Alan: So, anyway,.. Here we've got Abraham . . .

Phil: You're losing control of this.

Alan: I never had control of this.

John: That's an illusion of hope.

Alan: Yes, that a delusion of hope.

Charlie: Get your camels going in one direction, Al.

Alan: Like working with a herd of cats.

John: I thought it was a gaggle.

Alan: Here we've got Abraham called to serve. He's gone off and occupied a foreign country . . .

John: Keep trying!

Alan: Yup . . . he's joined the category of being a deceiver. We've perhaps all done it – one using another – either deceived ourselves or been deceived, and then the Lord afflicts Pharaoh because of Sarah, Abraham's wife. So Pharaoh calls Abraham, and says, "What is this that you have done to me?"

Ray: A venereal affliction?

Alan: One wonders.

John: Or ethereal.

Jack: It says "great plagues."

Alan: "What is this that you've done to me?" You read that and you wonder who could say that?

Charlie: We could say it as veterans.

Alan: "What is this that you have done to me?"

Linda: The country of Vietnam, the citizens, the people of Vietnam.

Alan: "What is this that you have done to me?"

Jack: The people of My Lai said that.

Phil: Can I ask a question? How does he find out it was his wife? It doesn't say that. He just assumed?

Charlie: Didn't he see them talking in the garden, and Pharaoh determined by the type of conversation that they were man and wife.

Phil: Oh. Right. There's some stuff missing in the extract.

Ken: But the anger. "What is this that you have done to me?"

Alan: What about the anger?

Russ: The lead-in says that Lord afflicted Pharaoh and his house with a great plague because of Sarah, Abraham's wife. And then Pharaoh asks, "What is this you have done to me?" Not giving God credit for afflicting him. Maybe because he was an atheist or whatever? They were Egyptians.

Charlie: They worshipped cats.

David: Cats never go in for that either.

John: Here is our shepherd. Cat got your tongue, Alan?

Ken: So you want to know about anger?

Alan: Please!

Ken: I got angry a number of times. It started to show up in the letters that the chaplain had to write to the families of the deceased troops.

Charlie: Oh, man.

Ken: Remember those things?

Charlie: Oh yeah.

Ken: I had to write them all the time for brigade. So I started to get angry. And it must have come out in the letters because I got a whole batch of them sent back saying, "You can't say this. You have to re-write them." From Saigon.

Phil: Because they were under the commander's signature, right?

Ken: That's right. I was writing them for the commander and he would just sign them and pass them on. They came back saying you can't say this stuff.

Alan: What were you saying? Do you remember?

Jack: "Your son died because somebody fucked up."

Ken: No, it wasn't quite as graphic as that. It was just something like, "We are sorry to inform you . . . we want you to know that we offer you our sympathies.' I remember in one I said, "but in a couple days they'll send a replacement and your son will be forgotten." Something like that.

Charlie: Yeah. That was pretty direct there.

John: "Started showing up!" An RPG letter!

Phil: You must have lost your "pastoral heart."

Ken: I was pissed. At one point I had a month, six weeks left and a guy by the name of B****** - guy from Philadelphia --he was at base camp and I was out in the boonies – I came in and got so angry. I kind of blew my cool and he was going to send me to the psych and then said, "Why don't we switch? You only got six weeks left. You come back here and I'll go out there. Change." But we didn't. I wonder what happened to (him). But that's what I mean about being angry. Another story. I got angry. I got sent to Washington after school; I got sent down to (Fort) Myers. That was the Christmas bombing year 1972. I had midnight mass at the Fort Myers with all the brass and the diplomatic corps. I'd been walking the halls of that chapel down there trying to figure out what to say that night to that crowd. You know – the Prince of Peace, and what do I do? I just got up and told the people that I spent two years, two Christmases in combat, and this was the saddest because of what was happening, and then I sat down. Well, I said a few other things, but then I sat down. Creighton Abrams was there; and Creighton Abrams came in to the sacristy and put his arms around me and said, "It is not a happy day for me either." He was chief of staff, I was pastor of the parish, and he was part of the parish.

Phil: I didn't know he was a Catholic.

Ken: He became a Catholic over there. His wife and kids were. Creighton Abrams was a rumpled . . . the antithesis of Westy.

Charlie: That's good.

Ken: Rumpled, friendly, very blunt. I got angry in different ways at different times.

Charlie: There's a sermon in there someplace.

Alan: Did you ever write those letters, Charlie?

Charlie: No, I think they nixed them in our place.

Ken: I had to write them all the time.

Alan: What about you, Jack?

Jack: I never had to write them.

Charlie: We were in the same unit.

Ken: We had lots of casualties . . . I brought some letters home.

John: You brought some home?

Ken: I got a letter from a family, a father wanting to know why his son was murdered. His son died in combat. I was there when he got killed. And I remember writing the father. I became friends with them. They came to see me when I was in Washington. They were living down in Virginia. But these letters were . . . you couldn't crank them out. You couldn't keep repeating the same thing and after a while . . . and we had a lot of casualties.

Alan: In this story of Abraham and Sarah and Pharaoh, is there a tragic character?

Ken: Sarah.

Alan: Sarah's not mentioned at all. She doesn't say anything. She's the silent character.

Charlie: Victims are usually silent, aren't they?

Phil: Tossed around like a football.

Alan: That's a good point, Charlie.

Charlie: Who speaks for the victim?

Alan: Or is the tragic character God?

Jack: In what way, Alan?

Alan: I don't know. Certainly the Lord had planned great things for Abraham and then Abraham goes off and does his own thing. He goes down to Egypt, deceived people, is deceived perhaps himself, and it isn't what God planned for him.

Phil: Yet God had to keep his promise.

Alan: God had to keep his promise in spite of all that. And at the end of all this, Abraham ends up blessed!

Jack: So God and Sarah were used.

Bruce: God is on a mission though. He can never be a victim. He can't be a victim and do all creation.

Russ: You're saying that . . .

Bruce: He said, "Who's the victim here? God was."

Linda: No, no.

Alan: Could God be the victim?

Bruce: Oh.

Jack: Well, if you take classic Christian theology, God was, in fact, the victim on the cross.

Bruce: No, he wasn't because he was the cause of that; he wasn't the effect of that.

Jack: O. K. We're different on that.

Russ: This is why I said earlier that if you take the collective assumptions on this particular panel, these kinds of statements can be challenged, because the text says what the text says. The line that I read earlier that God afflicted Pharaoh because of Sarah. And Pharaoh says to Abraham, "Why did you afflict me?" But that's taking it theologically. It's a perfectly good question from the text to ask "Was God the victim?" And people who do not impose Christian theology on the text can raise that kind of a question very legitimately, and in this panel they do. You need to read that knowing that, because when you listen to a Buddhist or a Jew or a Muslim they're in that. It's a very instructive text to us to let us see other points of view. Because maybe you or I never thought of all these things, and those thoughts need to be thought because these are people in the world just like us.

Jack: Well, whether or not you believe that God can be victimized, it certainly looks like, in this text, that some of the humans involved were attempting to take God for a ride.

David: For their own purposes.

Jack: Certainly the idea of using God for your own purposes is not unique.

Alan: That's a good way to put it. I don't think that there's any nation that goes off to war without the blessing of the cannons

Charlie: In this desperate time the Soviet Union even calls on God.

Linda: It seems to me that God's greatest gift to human beings is this idea of free will. It's the same thing with the promise to Abraham. God will keep God's promise regardless of how much we abuse the whatever gift it is that God has given us.

Charlie: I don't want to do that. I want God to rescue me from all the stupidity.

Linda: I have no doubt there are times throughout history, and I think this is one of those times, where God weeps with us in the insanity of our choices, of our abuse of free will, especially when its towards other human beings. Then again I haven't had the theological training you've all had.

Charlie: That ain't all bad!

John: Well, that explains it.

Ken: "Training" might be the right word; "knowledge" might be better to have.

Russ: You know, on the question of who is the tragic figure? Sarah and God seem to be in the place of the "have not's". Abraham and maybe Pharaoh in the place of the "haves." The "haves" and the "have not's" kind of came to mind as I thought about - someone said the victims never have a voice. When you read these texts, the plight of the victim is really quite hard. If you look at this, who is that victim?

Sacrifice

Excerpts from Genesis 22 and 23 (NRSV)

After these things God tested Abraham. He said to him, "Abraham!" And he said, "Here I am." He said, "Take your son, your only son Isaac, whom you love, and go to the land of Moriah, and offer him there as a burnt offering on one of the mountains that I shall show you." So Abraham rose early in the morning, saddled his donkey, and took two of his young men with him, and his son Isaac; he cut the wood for the burnt offering, and set out and went to the place in the distance that God had shown him. On the third day Abraham looked up and saw the place far away.

Then Abraham said to his young men, "Stay here with the donkey; the boy and I will go over there; we will worship, and then we will come back to you." Abraham took the wood of the burnt offering and laid it on his son Isaac, and he himself carried the fire and the knife. So the two of them walked on together.

Isaac said to his father Abraham, "Father!" And he said, "Here I am, my son." He said, "The fire and the wood are here, but where is the lamb for a burnt offering?" Abraham said, "God himself will provide the lamb for a burnt offering, my son." So the two of them walked on together. When they came to the place that God had shown him, Abraham built an altar there and laid the wood in order. He bound his son Isaac, and laid him on the altar, on top of the wood. Then Abraham reached out his hand and took the knife to kill his son.

But the angel of the Lord called to him from heaven, and said, "Abraham, Abraham!" And he said, "Here I am." He said, "Do not lay your hand on the boy or do anything to him; for now I know that you fear God, since you have not withheld your son, your only son, from me." And Abraham looked up and saw a ram, caught in a thicket by its horns. Abraham went and took the ram and offered it up as a burnt offering instead of his son. So Abraham called that place "The Lord will provide"; as it is said to this day, "On the mount of the Lord it shall be provided."

The angel of the Lord called to Abraham a second time from heaven, and said, "By myself I have sworn, says the Lord: Because you have done this, and have not withheld your son, your only son, I will indeed bless you, and I will make your offspring as numerous as the stars of heaven and as the sand that is on the seashore.

* * * * *

So Abraham returned to his young men, and they arose and went together to Beer-sheba; and Abraham lived at Beer-sheba.

* * * * *

Sarah lived one hundred twenty-seven years; this was the length of Sarah's life. And Sarah died at Kiriath-arba (that is, Hebron) in the land of Canaan.

* * * * *

Participating: Alan, Charlie, Bruce, David, Ray, Harvey, Jack, Jeff, Ken, Linda, Russ

* * * * *

Alan: This story of Abraham and Isaac raises a number of disturbing questions. I guess the first one revolves around this: are our blessings always secured by the slaughter of our children? And does that somehow resonate with anything that we have experienced looking at this Scripture with the lens, the eyes, of veterans?

Russ: I don't want to direct this away from our Vietnam experience, but my close friend, with whom I grew up, has a tentative project he intends to pose at Harvard Medical School, if he can be accepted, in which he intends to explore the idea that western civilization is based upon the sacrifice of children and this is one of the ideas, one of the texts – this text along with those of St. Augustine on the nature of original sin, Sigmund Freud, and Sophocles' Oedipus Rex, those major texts which have influenced western history. It's not a matter of taking lightly this text because of its huge impact on the way we think in Western civilization. I want to walk with my friend very carefully through this exercise he is about to enter in.

Jack: Well, it's a very big thing. It's not only the Christian component of Western Civilization. Obviously this is in the Jewish Scriptures. An interesting thing – in the Moslem Scriptures – in the Koran – you've got the same story except I think it's Ishmael who is offered up, so in each culture you have the ancestor of the race who, in this parallel story, is offered up to God and almost sacrificed. And this is paralleled in the Christian narrative; certainly some people look at the experience of Christ going to the cross as something where there is free will; and Jesus makes a decision; and, yes, there is offering on the cross. But Jesus kind of does it, and the chief priests and the Romans have their parts to play and so forth. But there is another Christian strain that sees the whole thing very much like this: that now it is God in the place of Abraham and it is Jesus in the place of Isaac – and Jesus is basically powerless - and God sacrifices God's son – and in that narrative, the sacrifice goes all the way though – nobody stops it. So it certainly is a very powerful narrative in the three major religions.

Harvey: I've thought about this story a great deal from a number of different perspectives. From the standpoint of a work of story telling it is as perfect a story as I think has ever been written – in terms of its power and its impact. One of the qualities of its greatness is that it reveals two sides; and today, in this group, I cannot help but think in light of what I've heard, I sense that there many "Isaacs" around the table with me. One of the things that isn't addressed in the actual text is how did Isaac feel after this. How did he feel after his father said, "Don't worry. I'll take care of the ram." And bound him on the altar of sacrifice. Isaac was not foolish. He knew what was coming. This was his own father. In an earlier comment, Ray was talking about safety and peace – when we were trying to describe Eden metaphorically as that sense of trust that a child, a little girl has when she jumps into her father's arms. That to me is Eden - that sense of safety, well-being, and peace. And risklessness. This is the opposite. This is where you were proud to do your duty; you were doing what you thought was right; you were obeying your father, and he's taking you on the mountain to kill you.

Alan: I couldn't help read this without thinking of you, Bruce, as a drill sergeant. It's sort of an Abraham figure with these little Isaacs, and then you were talking about seeing their names listed on the Wall. But on the other hand, you also, in your own time, had a drill sergeant who tried to prepare you to go over there and you came back. Do you feel that tension?

Bruce: Yeah. A lot of guilt. A lot of guilt came from that experience simply because . . . I was a basket case when it happened – like I mentioned before – each one of those people – could I have done something else, could I have said something else, or did I miss something in the training? Was I slack somewhere? All things that came back. And it's like a medic; medics in Vietnam who were expected to perform major heart surgery on the battlefield or whatever. And really they were trying to stop the bleeding. A lot of them – I meet them all the time – have this terrible guilt for thinking that they should have done more to save lives.

Russ: There's such an effort to save Abraham that I find it necessary to say that had I been in the position I would have told God he could go to hell or he could send me to hell, but I would not raise a knife against my son.

Linda: Amen.

Russ: That needs to be said, and now I'm not saying there are not other things about the story that are important, but I think I could not take seriously an order to slaughter my son.

Linda: But then people took orders to kill other people's sons.

Jack: There are people who hear the voice of God telling them to go out and kill somebody else. There have been trials. Generally that gets them off on grounds of insanity. We tend to lock people like that up.

Charlie: Depends on the context.

Jack: Except in war.

Charlie: And then they are highly decorated!

Jack: Yes.

Charlie: I can think of maybe one guy who directly caused the death of his son by his orders in Vietnam, but that's a unique case. On this text, we were taught to translate contextually. I see a lot of eisegesis in what we do here with the text. I don't know if you want to own that, but I've got to own it. But, if we're going to interpret it experientially, and I thing we need to say we're doing that, I interpret that experientially we're everybody in that place, in that Scripture – we're Abraham, we're Isaac, and sometimes I think we're the poor little sheep that got trapped in that thicket. Because we had no control – some poor guys had no control over what was going to happen to them – they had a fantasy – drills tried to teach that whatever the situation was they could cope with it. But, you knew, when a big old rocket comes down and hits you in the head, you can't do a damn thing about it. In a tenth of a second you're gone!

Russ: There's another thing – the women – not consulting Sarah. Isaac was as much Sarah's son as he was Abraham's son. Or not consulting of Hagar about Ishmael.

Charlie: You trying to make me feel guilty now?

Russ: What?

Charlie: Trying to make me feel guilty, or not feel guilty?

Russ: Do I feel guilty?

Charlie: No, trying to make me feel guiltier?

Russ: No, I'm not trying to make you guilty. I'm simply saying that not to consider another human being who has every much a right – and if that makes me a feminist so be it. A woman has much right to the value of their children as the father. And that is missing from the story whether it's in the holy Koran or Genesis 22.

Harvey: I just think that is an absolutely profound point and I'd like to reiterate – forgive me for doing so – do the people here feel like Isaac? Can you imagine how Isaac felt towards his father – the authority figure – after the incident? Because I mean I'm over here – if God said to me you have to raise a knife to your child, I'd say, "Do what you will with me." What was Isaac's relationship, your relationship with your father country, society?

Charlie: Real strained.

Harvey: I bet.

Ray: I put this in a slightly different context. I think Phil knows where I'm going with this, but one of the things that I discovered quite recently as a result of my own hitting the wall was this fact - we were caught in an ambush situation in a convoy and something that I always had with me was my Yashica 35 mm camera. I took pictures of everything; I loved taking pictures of the countryside; I thought it was one of the most lush, most beautiful pieces of property on all of creation – except for the war. And we got stopped. I confused that story as I thought about it, as it flashed back to me – but in looking at the pictures – there was a little boy on the side of the road who was joined by his sister – almost immediately after I took the picture of the boy – well, I took a picture of the boy and the girl together. No more had I set the camera down when out of the corner of my eye I saw the boy take a - I mean we're talking a little boy about so high – something out from behind him that I interpreted to be a grenade – simultaneously fire stated coming from the wood line – and I took a twelve gauge, sawed-off shotgun – short stock – and blew these two kids apart – and the guilt I feel as a result of that is almost unbearable. Two weeks ago I was with my therapist – and he asked me to bring these pictures in – pictures that I had looked at several times over the course of the last thirty years – but it had never hit me. And as he looked at the pictures – he could see – to put it in this context – Sarah standing in the background. There was a woman behind the children slightly lower in terms of the terrain than they were – and the feeling of pain after all that – and I'm still not able to cry over that – It hasn't got to that point yet. But the whole idea of the sacrifice of children, whether it was we as, I want to say, adolescent children being sent off to perhaps die, which many did, at the request of our forefathers who were calling us into this mess. When he pointed out to me the woman in the background the horror of what I did hit me that much harder, because she saw what I believe to be her two children - from a distance from myself to the easel – be taken apart by – I don't know how many times I pumped that shotgun – it was probably out of casings by the time I finished – but double-ought buck will do a hell of a job on people – on anything. And this story, this story brings such pain to me that it's something . . . I don't know . . . Sometimes I kind of think we hold on to our pain because it's something that's sacred to us. We don't let it go. We don't allow ourselves that opportunity to cry. The therapist said to me, "You may never be able to grieve that loss – that moment." But the pain of reading this passage, and every time I read this passage when it comes up in the lectionary – all the time it seems – and being a lectionary preacher, I'll tell you what, more that one time, on more than one occasion, I sure as hell haven't wanted to preach on this text. The Sunday after I arrived in Richmond, the week after I was divorced, what should be the theme? The whole theme of divorce, and I got hit smack between the eyes. And that's the way this passage hits me. Especially seeing in my own eyes my own granddaughter at that same age.

Alan: One of the things that Ray mentions, and perhaps even illustrates, that I feel that I lost was the ability to read a passage like this one and see the big picture. Immediately, for me, everything becomes so personal. Maybe we did go there as sacrificial lambs or something like that. Or fulfilled some sort of a role. But I know when I got there in '71-'72 we were still killing children. It was a situation where you wouldn't even let a child get near you. One of the things we were expected to do – if a child got near you – you pulled out your weapon. If you stopped your jeep on a street, you pulled out your weapon and you kept ranging back and forth to keep any child from coming near the jeep, near the vehicle; otherwise they might throw in a charge or something. Certainly if they could get close enough they'd steal the wristwatch off your hand; they'd steal anything that was not tied down in the jeep. And you read a passage like this – and for those of us that preach every Sunday – there are lots of times where I have to read the Scriptures and then I have to almost take a day to go through the images that it brings up and my own personal shit, so to speak, before I can even say, "O.K., how will I preach this?" Because you can't preach what you just said to a congregation, even though they should probably hear it. You would devastate the little old ladies in the front pew! Get a call from the bishop. It would just be too much.

Jack: And yet it's for want of devastation that the 'little old ladies" keep electing people who send boys off to war.

Alan: Yes.

David: The worst day of my life wasn't in Vietnam. It was in 1991, when a little six-year-old girl in the congregation where I was serving was killed by a drunk driver. She'd always been the one who always sat next to me when I did the children's story in church – my youngest daughter's first friend when we arrived there four years before that. You asked if we're still sacrificing children to advance our own – or something like that --

Alan: Blessings.

David: After that some of us did some organizing to try and address the problem of drunk drivers around there. Because that's still a Wild West town! It's part of the culture. And I guess it was two months later that the mayor told the police chief to tell his guys to stop writing so many drunk driving tickets because they were scaring away business in town. I'd like to go back someday to Vietnam to see it at peace, but I don't think I ever want to go back to that place, because that broke my heart.

Jeff: Can I interject something about the passage? I've got a lot of faith in my God and a lot of trust in my God, but I still have to wonder about a God who would order his ardent followers to kill their kids as a test of faith, even if he planned on not letting it go through. The anguish he must have caused Abraham. The anguish he caused Isaac. You've got to sometimes question and doubt the love of a God that would do that; and yet at the same time, I turn around and listen to stories like this, and then I wonder about the parents who would send their children to do it. And in your story and the picture I would wonder about the mom, knowing what the kids were going to do, letting them do it. Yeah, I think we earn a lot of our blessings – but somehow – when the kids are sacrificed you've got to wonder about the reasons.

Linda: I've always wondered – the question of what did Isaac do after that. And certainly if I had any trust in my government before I went – and I did because I believed what we were doing was right – I had virtually none when I came back. A friend of mine – she said, "I'm surprised you still cry when you hear some patriotic songs." I said, "It's true – the emotion that you see is typically the same, but it's for very, very different reasons." The tears I now cry, they are of pain and betrayal. I saw too many people sacrificed for . . . there's no reason for this; it's just a test of faith. There's no reason given here, and I just see too many tests in too many places in different parts of the world.

Alan: You notice that at the end of the passage that Abraham comes down from the mountain and back to the lads alone. Isaac is not with him.

Linda: I wouldn't be either! I would have run like hell someplace else.

David: It may be, I think you used the term, eisegesis. But let me preface that, my office administrator at my church – her parents were orthodox Jews though they raised her reformed, and then went back to their orthodox synagogue afterward – and we have kind of an interesting relationship – her father and I – because he was my source of useful obscure, stuff to put in sermons. In Jewish interpretation of scripture – the way the rabbis did it – he did show me something once that was on this passage. And the take of the rabbis that he was quoting from – I can't remember their names, but it was way back when – was that Abraham would not have [found it odd], given the surroundings of the time – an old Canaanite thing – that sacrificing your first born was real popular to earn the favor of your god. At that time Abraham might not had believed it was God asking him had God asked for anything less. And so to train him that we don't do this, he had to take him through the depths and up to the heights and then stop him. I don't know. That doesn't make it easier for me to read the story, but it shows that somebody else had been struggling with this too, for a long, long time because this was somebody back over 500 years ago that had done this.

Russ: To expand on that, somehow as an Abilene Christian, I never dreamed that I would take textual criticism seriously; however, I'm totally contaminated! These Genesis texts were probably – scholarship says – that these texts probably were somewhat near the same date, time and authorship as the 7th century prophets; and when you read certainly Micah and some of the others, you find that child sacrifice was one of the things they were speaking our against. And so Abraham – and your point from the rabbis is well taken – that child sacrifice was not a strange thing, even in Israel, and that's why the prophets were having to say these things to Israel – not to sacrifice children. So, to me that appreciation of textual criticism has given me the freedom to see the text somewhat like the rabbi said, though I certainly go with Micah, rather than the traditional understanding of Abraham's faith..

Jack: In a sense its almost as if the liberals have a much easier time with this than the conservatives if you define a liberal as somebody who would look at the story essentially as really like a parable – a story whose authenticity doesn't really matter but it's a story that there to make a point and you look – the main point really is that it's good to give yourself and everything you have whole-heartedly to God, and that's the point; then you take the point and disregard the rest of the story and move on. But if you're more conservative and you looking at this as something that actually happened and these were real people, then you get caught up in all of these things and you get much more out of it than simply "the point." And I think that's what we're struggling with from the perspective of the conservatives here treating this whole thing as a real story and really getting into at as a real thing. It sure would be a lot easier to say, "Here's the point. Let's move on!"

Ray: Isn't it like most of our folks - and maybe this is too broad a statement - but most of our folks at least within the Protestant tradition have no regard for Good Friday. They go from Maundy Thursday – if they're there – or else you have your "C" and "E's" – then they just come for Easter – the hell with Good Friday – what was so good about it if somebody got killed? They totally ignore the depth and the meaning of what has taken place. You know they want resurrection without death; they want eternity without life as we know it.

Alan: There's another point of view. Take Abraham as a good, righteous man, as he is presented in the scriptures. He has received the promise of a blessing from God. He knows that his very survival in a strange land depends upon obedience to the God who is offering him protection, so the God makes this demand, and he knows that the entire good of his posterity depends upon his obeying God. As a good, righteous man, he's going to obey God but also he's going to do this terrible thing and kill his child. Imagine the welter of emotions when you do things that you know are outside the pale, solely so you can survive. Anyone want to pick up on that?

Jeff: Can I go back a topic just to say something to Russ? You know, Russ, I can believe in textual criticism and when scholarship says it was written. If this God that we love and trust hadn't required the death of his own son then I could very easily put this into the category, as the liberals do, of an interesting story. But I have to believe in the truth of this actually happening because God in fact did require the sacrifice of his own son, so in this case textual criticism be damned.

Russ: Well, I think Caiaphas is responsible in a very direct way, rather than God so much. That's not textual criticism.

Linda: Something that you said reminds me of – please correct me if I'm wrong on this – but I was under the impression that it was not unusual for some mothers to be coerced – or invited – to sacrifice their children or put their children in harm's way or danger for preciously that which we were talking about, meaning if they've got six kids, they were told this one will do this or we'll kill them all. I know I've read reports that indicated this. And I know I've talked with people in intelligence situations who said this was not unusual, so what you're saying about survival and what you're saying about how they could do that – you're given a choice – you lose all of your kids or you put one or two in harm's way and you can save the others.

Charlie: It's a Vietnamese Sophie's Choice.

Jack: When I was a boy in Malaysia people remembered the Japanese soldiers and the same kind of thing, you know, tossing babies up on a bayonet and essentially giving parents a choice – pick one or I'll kill them both.

David: It happened in Vietnam too. All the people I talked to – they may not have liked us being there and they didn't want the French there, but they despised the Japanese because of their memories of World War Two.

Bruce: I think it's interesting, and I'm sure that some people here may not want to hear this, it's interesting that the same year they brought our kids home from Vietnam they legalized abortion and we're sitting here talking about killing kids and I'm not in any way an activist against abortion, but it's just the thought of the millions of babies that have been killed since this stupid law – our sick society has been killing babies in the womb.

Charlie: I'll just piggyback on that. Some kids, some older kids were going though some breast-beating when I was taking a course with the Bible chair at the University of Kansas. Our professor of sociology of religion there looked like he could be the lead biker in Hell's Angels, and he had a face -- you would never argue with this guy. He was the chief peacemaker on campus – the students were shooting there; I saw the bullet holes in two-inch plate glass – that wasn't B-B guns – he'd walk the line and do peace. He asked me one day what was wrong, and I told him I felt so terrible about all this stuff – about all the guys we lost in Vietnam. And he said, "That's all politics. If the people in this country really cared about children, they would make them wear helmets when they're doing motorcycles; they would do a lot of other stuff – It's just like what's up in front today, but it's not a really, deep, whole-hearted concern for children – it's just kind the issue that's going to get the vote, going to get the power; and they really don't care about it." That didn't help my cynicism a whole lot.

Russ: If children were really intrinsically valuable across our society a child's life would be valued from conception.

Charlie: Right

Russ: Whoever said that life begins at conception, I go with that, and that would certainly modify a lot of sexual behavior; it certainly would impact on rampart abortion for every . . . that kind of thing . . .if children were valued as intrinsically and ultimately valuable.

Linda: But they be valued throughout their whole life, Russ.

Charlie: Yeah. Right.

Linda: I mean to bring a child into abject poverty where they have nothing, no life or anything, into an abusive situation – that's, I think, as sinful as taking a child in the womb. There's got to be a way to get children health care and education and those things, and have it guaranteed that they will be taken care of; otherwise, I'm not exactly sure where I stand there.

Jack: Well, there's an interesting study that was reported in the local newspaper around Sunday that somebody got very curious about our attitudes towards children. This is way off your topic, Alan, but what the heck! They did a study of the laws and policies in all fifty states, and those states which had the most restrictive view toward abortion also were the states that, by just about every other indicator, made it hard for people to have children, hard for people to bring up children, hard for people to take care of children, lowest welfare payments for children – you know, every other indicator. These were the states that, judged by the laws and policies, cared the least about children. Now that doesn't say anything in terms of the relative morality of abortion or about how it ties into this thing. Just for the record, so that nobody imagines we have a unanimous perspective on this, I've had involvement on abortion in the other direction. I think, like Bruce, that it's not something I have a whole lot of energy about at this point, but I think if we decided we wanted to spend the time on a discussion, we could have a discussion on both sides, but I don't think that's what this is about.

David: Just so it's on your tape . . .

Charlie: This on tape?

David: You're in trouble now! Just so it's on your tape, I have to say I know it's been a long time interpretation that the price had to be paid to God, because of God's justice therefore etc., etc. But I don't think the Bible show us is that God demands the sacrifice of his son; I don't think it says that. It takes a long time to talk around that one, but I think it at least should be said that there's a range of opinion present on that subject.

Charlie: God requires mercy, not sacrifice.

David: Yeah. And as another fellow put it, God is not a child abuser.

Jack: If you believe in the total humanity of Christ as well as the divinity of Christ, then Christ had free will until the very last moment to not go through with this thing; it wasn't God who killed him.

David: "God required . . ." When people pin me on this, I say what God needed, required, was faithfulness. Faithfulness had its own consequences but it was the people that supplied the consequences. God would have been quite happy if everybody had said, "Well, let's forget this and go home instead." I think it could have been accomplished that way too because I don't think there are limits on the power of God. It didn't take the death and the blood to do it. It was people that required death. God chose to use that nonetheless, but it wasn't God who required death.

Jack: Herod made decisions; the chief priest made decisions.

Russ: I'd like to come back to the question he raised there because I would not have Genesis 22 extracted from the text. Neither would I have the final verse of Psalm 137 taken out of the text, the one which makes people happy for bashing Babylonian babies heads against the rock. I'm horrified by just reading about it. By the way in the lectionary, the verse is . . .

Ray: Is taken out.

Russ: Omitted from the reading. And I would not have the text removed that tells how Elijah killed 450 prophets with whom he disagreed. I suspect that I could find 450 preachers in Dallas that I disagreed with – but I don't want to get started. But I don't try to take it out of the text because somehow, - and in the call of Abraham, with him being the scoundrel that he turned out to be - some how there is something about God that is communicated, even if those texts are totally offensive and obnoxious for me. Even if they're not, I'm willing to suspend what I can't understand because the text is extremely important to me. I do say that Jesus stands in judgment of the text; and that's my hermeneutic – but slashing and burning those texts . . .

David: I try to force myself to preach the ones I hate in an exercise of "let's deal with what's there!" As I tell other people, you can't take it out of context. I'm not going to rip the pieces out that bug me.

Russ: That's what this exercise is about tonight.

Harvey: I'd like to say as an addendum to what I said before, when I was agreeing with Russ, which was if God said kill, and I was in a similar situation I would just say, "God, look, I'm trying to do the best I can – but I've got to draw the line there and I'll take the consequences." I did not foresee or imagine . . . and probably would not accept that. It gives me the opportunity to say this now. Had I known, Ray, what you went through . . . what I will say is that I hope, I hope that your friends in faith – people who care about you and others who were in similar situations – as there were many – yours is a case that relates right into this -- I hope that there is some sanctuary, indeed awareness that you were faced with a trial where your hand wasn't stayed, where there wasn't a ram. I certainly don't think less of you for that. I'm deeply sorry that you were in that situation. Because until you shared your story, I thought this was as a great a trial as there is; and then I hear yours. And I say, "Well, there it is." And so I want to say that my statement, "No, I wouldn't do it," is cavalier, and based on not being in that situation. I expect I would have done exactly the same thing that you did. I expect that I would find the pain of that as unbearable as you have. At the same time, I hope that ultimately that Scripture can provide some step back toward healing, because it is a measure of how great a trial you have been put through; I really hope and pray for you that healing will come.

Ray: One of the things, and this is an extension beyond that passage and our subject, is this. I have said that my daughter had a stillborn son. This was – I don't know the exact date – but I may have written it on the pictures of the kids and I have the pictures of those kids. My daughter was faced with a very difficult choice because she was about twenty-four weeks along.

In the state of North Carolina, anything past twenty weeks you cannot perform an abortion. My daughter went for a sonogram; and they could not find the baby. In fact, the reason why was that there was no amniotic fluid. They injected amniotic fluid into the womb, and the baby started to thrash and do all sorts of things – and I can only imagine what that must have felt like to my daughter. The doctor gave her an option because in the examination of the sonogram and all of that – this baby was in essence dead because there was no amniotic fluid present. I never learned until that point that it's the baby that produces the amniotic fluid – I was totally unaware of that. So she was faced with the harsh reality of deciding whether or not to terminate the pregnancy. This doctor put himself in jeopardy by saying that she was only nineteen weeks along to perform this service, so that she should not have to carry this child full term knowing that the child was either dead or not viable. The other factor was that the placenta was right across the cervix, so if she had gone into delivery stage, she would have bled to death before anything could have been done. So she and I talked on the phone extensively – at great length – along with her mother – and I said, "I can't make the decision for you. It is yours to make alone. I can only say that in whatever you decide I will support you 100%." She did not know – she made the decision that she would have the pregnancy terminated. Out of my own pain I flew down, unbeknownst to her, and walked into her room at midnight. Her husband and she were there and I stayed with them through the delivery process and this – I mean I have pictures of the baby – he was in essence purple because the skin is so translucent at that point that all the capillaries and everything else just show the blood – but here was an absolutely beautiful little baby boy fully formed, but who had absolutely no chance of life whatsoever. The kidneys had not developed; the digestive track had not developed; both opening were closed - the urinary as we as the rectal; because there was no amniotic fluid, the lungs hadn't developed. And I thought as that child was delivered, and it was forty years to the day for that doctor that his mother went through the same process and it was thirty years, within a few days, that I went through my experience in Vietnam. And as this baby was laid on my daughter's stomach, it was the only time that I took of my fatherly hat and said, "Can we say a little prayer?" And based on my son-in-law's beliefs, being in the Church of Christ, that you wait until the child is old enough to decide for himself to be baptized or not; within my own heart, within my own mind, within my own prayer, I said a baptismal prayer for that child. And the pain as a result of what happened this past February and all of this shit coming to the forefront – it all ties together - the sacrifices that we have to make in life at times and the pain that brings. We celebrated his life. She's pregnant again. She's doing very well and is due to give birth; and I'm so happy for them, as well as for me. I have to be honest – but you know the pain of the reality of all that is such that placing ourselves in Isaac's and Sarah's position, it just overwhelms me.

Jack: There's a theme in here that hasn't been picked up on. It just struck me looking at this. At the beginning, when Abraham is first receiving the command from God, the command is to Abraham to take Isaac and go forth into the land of Moriah, the "land of seeing." Presumably at that moment then, they are not in the "land of seeing." They're in the "land of non-seeing." At the moment of seeing the ram -- Abraham lifted up his eyes, and saw the ram -- therefore after offering up the ram, Abraham called that place "God will provide" [in another translation "God sees"]. And you have the contrast between the two times – the one command of God takes place in the "land of non-seeing," and the command of God to stay his hand takes place in the "land of seeing." That strikes me as very powerful.

Bruce: It's a statement of the tremendous faith that Abraham had because in the middle of that it says, "God will see for himself." That's where Abraham put it. All in God's hands. "God will see for himself for the lamb for offering-up."

Jack: Mmmmhh.

Bruce: So this is really a tremendous statement. And, Russ, your comment on Sarah, I've been thinking about that. I've always thought – because I thought about that too – the bigger picture – what was she doing when this old man was taking her kid to stab him, what was she thinking? I've always had this picture in my mind of this woman who had tremendous faith, that she had faith that her man; and, being submitted to her husband, she trusted that he heard from God. That was her place as a woman of God, and that was her faith. So he had faith. She had faith. This is a story of faith because he went up that hill and he knew in his mind that he wasn't going to kill his kid. He had that much faith.

Jack: I don't get that from the story.

Bruce: "God will see for himself for the lamb for offering-up." I don't think he was a liar. I think he had enough faith that God would handle the circumstances and that he would come back with his son because he does say, "We'll be back." In other translations, he tells the lads you guts wait here and we'll come back. It doesn't say, "I'll come back." Even though it does say that he came back alone. It does say, "We'll come back."

Russ: You may be correct about Abraham. You may be correct about Sarah. You may be correct about God. But I don't have that kind of faith, and I don't want anybody to think that I have that kind of faith, because I don't. And I would think that compassion for my son has to convey whatever kind of faith I have, and I just don't have that kind of faith. I'm sorry.

Alan: You mentioned this idea of God sees. I read this and I think, "Here's Abraham and he has got to make a choice." He's in a situation where it seems to me he has to make a bad choice. I think we all found ourselves – as Ray has perhaps illustrated and some of the rest of us have illustrated – in situations where we had to make bad choices or certainly destructive choices, and there was no ram in the thicket at the point. I find myself with a little ambivalent feeling about whether or not, at those moments, God was seeing what I was doing. There is part of me that wants to maintain the image of the overwhelming goodness of God that would provide a ram in the thicket, but there's part of me that says I find comfort in the idea of a God that sees, because I find no comfort in a God that does not see. I find comfort in a God that sees and will allow the bad choices to be made. I've thought often of all the times, all the places, that you read about God being sought to "come to the aid" of our side in battle, whichever side it might be. I've come to the conclusion that, in warfare or in some of these bad choices, I will be more than happy if I can proclaim that God is neutral – but present. And I could preach that. And I think I could sustain it theologically.

Harvey: It's interesting that if one were to preach that God is neutral but present, I think one could make a very convincing argument that warfare is not consistent with God's wish for us to solve problems. So Alan may be headed in a good, productive direction.

David: I don't think you'll get much argument.

Charlie: What do we do with our own hypocrisy is a part of the problem and we've got a whole bunch of other baggage to go with that.

Russ: In this imperfect world that we live in, I certainly prefer the Socratic method over the one that I saw happening which brought us into that war, and a lot of other conflicts.

Charlie: I do too, but you know, like the guy in Comic Relief, I'd rather talk it over with those guys but number one, they're shooting at me! And, number two, I don't speak Vietnamese. So what choices do we have there?

Russ: Well, I'll be glad for them to do sophomore history in college before they do anything.

Charlie: Well, when you're up to your ass in alligators, I . . .

Russ: In 1956, we weren't up to our ass in alligators.

David: We need to study a little more.

Charlie: I don't have any control over that. As my grandkids say, "I'm just a kid!"

Russ: I'm talking about Eisenhower. He was not "just a kid."

Charlie: But I don't have any control over Eisenhower.

Russ: But he had control over the decisions that he made.

Charlie: Yes, but I've got to live with his bad decisions!

Ken: Can we forgive the Abrahams for their bad decisions?

Charlie: I'm working on it, but it's really tough, really tough.

Harvey: To take Alan's idea, suggestion that God is neutral but present, my interpretation of the policy that got us into Vietnam was that God was not neutral, but that God abhorred communism because it was atheistic, that Vietnam was a domino that was going to hit another domino; but all along God was on our side, not neutral, not neutral.

Bruce: That's what you believe.

Harvey: No, that's what I believe our leaders believed. I believe that if our leaders believed that God was neutral but present as it related to what we should do about things in Southeast Asia, you guys would never have gotten there.

Bruce: War is the result of man's free will. Somebody's already said that, and it's one thing about us the God will never tamper with.

Charlie: Right.

Jack: Free will. And part of that free will has to be the matter of discerning that spirits, and I would suspect that most of us here in this room, if at some darkest point of our lives, heard a voice that claimed to be the voice of God that said take your son and go up on the mountain and kill him, we would determine that that was not the voice of God. And the point that I wanted to make with this thing on "seeing" was that this voice of God took place in the "darkness" but that the ram event took place at the place of "seeing." The son was saved at the place of "seeing." The son's death was commanded in the place of "darkness."

Russ: In your own life you've told about something you wrote – your father had a letter or something and read it – you said it sounded O.K., but you wouldn't say it today.

Jack: That radio broadcast.

Russ: O.K. Whatever it was – so that was the land, at least, of seeing less than you see today. And, yes, I suspect there was a time in my life when I might have heard the voice of God differently that I hear it today. Or my response to the voice of God today might be different that it would be twenty or thirty years ago. But I'm responsible for being where I am and in what I have said this evening – the best I could do today. Ten years from now, if the God lets me live so long, I would hope that I would have greater seeing than I have today. I live in that hope. And I want to share the seeing that I have!

Alan: One of the points that I might just touch upon is that while we might have been the Isaacs a number of years ago, we have certainly aged, and we are now at the point perhaps of being Abrahams. And it is time to sacrifice our own children. Now both Bruce and I have children in the military. I don't know about you, Bruce, but that gives me nightmares sometimes. Because I wonder - - - now my son-in-law was already sent to participate over in the Gulf, over the fly zone, and he was over for the Bosnia thing, and most recently he was in Turkey – and I just sort of wonder what they're going to be called upon to do.

Ken: What they are going to be called upon to do, and what responsibility and how do we exercise it to be part of the decision process leading up to what they are called upon to do, because if we criticized the Abrahams when we were Isaacs for thinking maybe – I'd like to think that they thought God was on our side – I'm more concerned that they were more concerned about oil and trade and other stuff.

Harvey: That's even worse.

Ken: Yes, that's what I mean!. I'd go for the first one! But how do we exercise that responsibility. Maybe around this table is one thing, but how do we do that in other places?

Charlie: How much control did Eisenhower have? I feel like he was in the north woods. I feel I've got about as much control as I do peeing on a forest fire.

Harvey: Can I just respond? If I'm extrapolating, Alan, from what you said about a neutral God who is present. I guess that if one looks at human free will as being the source of some kind of

-- it makes me wonder about how one views Abraham then in the original story because aren't we confronted with all the other Abrahams? All the parents who through history who send their sons off to be killed because God told them that was the right thing to do? But if God was neutral, then Abraham of his own free will could be saying, "You know, Isaac, let's stay here tonight." So I'm having a hard time reconciling your theological outlook, which I find very attractive, with this story, and since I'm over here in feeling I don't have this kind of faith – if we call it faith – that Abraham did – I prefer your theology over Abraham's.

David: I think that God is neutral but I don't think God is uninterested in this. In another place God says, "I set before you this day, life and death; therefore, choose life." Please. That's what God is doing in this neutral situation.

Harvey: Where's that?

Alan: Deuteronomy.

David: Hang on . . .

Harvey: But I don't see God saying it here.

Alan: No, not here.

David: That's why it's dangerous just to read one passage.

Charlie: Well, you can get yourself out of the philosophical dilemma if you believe in progressive revelation, but that doesn't help my guts out.

Alan: That's it. The head stuff is one thing, but if you've been in a situation where you've had to confront the bad choices and the reality of evil, then you've come against the terrible, the awesome truth of what we might call the "unknowability" of

God and for people who like to dot every "i", it's very frustrating that we can't know, with a great deal of certainty, God. That's why I'm willing to settle, as I said, for God's presence, which I don't interpret as an unfriendly presence. Everything that I read in Scripture pretty much ends up with a God of compassion, a God of mercy, a God of joy, a God of tears. I'm perfectly willing to accept that when I was killing people that God was neutral but crying – with the people I was killing, and with me – even if I was not. I was having a good time frankly.

Jack: Alan, if you were in the place of Abraham in this story, with the belief you've expressed about God, and you heard this voice telling you to take your son up on a mountainside and sacrifice him, would you believe that voice you heard was the voice of God?

Alan: No, I would not. Based upon my life experience, I cannot conceive that the God of creation would demand destruction, that the God of life would demand death. That does not compute with my understanding of the scriptures.

Bruce: That's the New Covenant.

Alan: Yes. Yet, if you put me in a situation where survival is at point – my survival – I'm well trained – I might react the same way I did twenty-five, twenty-seven years ago. I'd like to think that I wouldn't, but we all got a chance to look into the heart of evil, and who among us could say we wouldn't?

Jack: Perhaps part of that heart of evil is, in the midst of darkness, to hear the dark voice that is presented here and to imagine that that dark voice is the voice of God.

Apocalypse: Then and Now

Excepts from Genesis 6, 7, 8, and 9 (NRSV)

The Lord saw that the wickedness of humankind was great in the earth, and that every inclination of the thoughts of their hearts was only evil continually. And the Lord was sorry that he had made humankind on the earth, and it grieved him to his heart. So the Lord said, "I will blot out from the earth the human beings I have created—people together with animals and creeping things and birds of the air, for I am sorry that I have made them." But Noah found favor in the sight of the Lord. Noah was a righteous, wholehearted man in his generation. In accord with God did Noah walk . . .

And God said to Noah, "I have determined to make an end of all flesh, for the earth is filled with violence because of them; now I am going to destroy them along with the earth. Make yourself an ark of cypress wood; make rooms in the ark, and cover it inside and out with pitch . . .

For my part, I am going to bring a flood of waters on the earth, to destroy from under heaven all flesh in which is the breath of life; everything that is on the earth shall die. But I will establish my covenant with you; and you shall come into the ark, you, your sons, your wife, and your sons' wives with you. And of every living thing, of all flesh, you shall bring two of every kind into the ark, to keep them alive with you; they shall be male and female...

They went into the ark with Noah, two and two of all flesh in which there was the breath of life. And those that entered, male and female of all flesh, went in as God had commanded him; and the Lord shut him in. The flood continued forty days on the earth; and the waters increased, and bore up the ark, and it rose high above the earth. The waters swelled and increased greatly on the earth; and the ark floated on the face of the waters...

And all flesh died that moved on the earth, birds, domestic animals, wild animals, all swarming creatures that swarm on the earth, and all human beings; everything on dry land in whose nostrils was the breath of life died...

But God remembered Noah and all the wild animals and all the domestic animals that were with him in the ark. And God made a wind blow over the earth, and the waters subsided...

Then God said to Noah, "Go out of the ark, you and your wife, and your sons and your sons' wives with you. Bring out with you every living thing that is with you of all flesh—birds and animals and every creeping thing that creeps on the earth—so that they may abound on the earth, and be fruitful and multiply on the earth." Then Noah built an altar to the Lord, and took of every clean animal and of every clean bird, and offered burnt offerings on the altar. And when the Lord smelled the pleasing odor, the Lord said in his heart, "I will never again curse the ground because of humankind, for the inclination of the human heart is evil from youth; nor will I ever again destroy every living creature as I have done...

God said, "This is the sign of the covenant that I make between me and you and every living creature that is with you, for all future generations: I have set my bow in the clouds, and it shall be a sign of the covenant between me and the earth...

Noah, a man of the soil, was the first to plant a vineyard. He drank some of the wine and became drunk, and he lay uncovered in his tent. And Ham, the father of Canaan, saw the nakedness of his father, and told his two brothers outside. Then Shem and Japheth took a garment, laid it on both their shoulders, and walked backward and covered the nakedness of their father; their faces were turned away, and they did not see their father's nakedness. When Noah awoke from his wine and knew what his youngest son had done to him, he said, "Cursed be Canaan; lowest of slaves shall he be to his brothers."

* * * * *

Participating: Alan, Charlie, David, Ray, Harvey, Jack, John, Ken, Linda, Phil, Russ

Alan: The first question that I have to ask coming out of this particular passage - as I read it and contemplated it, I was thinking of you, David, working in the supply corps - this must have been one awful supply problem? How would you . . .

David: That thought entered my mind.

Alan: Well, what do you think about the supply problem Noah had?

David: I still agree with Bill Crosby's question, "Who is going to clean up after all this?"

Linda: Yeah. Who's going to clean up that mess down there?

Jack: Well, it would be one thing to supply the herbivores that are on the ark and that would be a big enough problem; but how do you supply the carnivores, or is the supply already there?

Alan: This assumption that's always made is that things just happen; but behind any kind of operation there's an organization.

Phil: You hope.

Alan: Yes, we hope. We read this passage from Genesis and we sort of skip over the miracle behind the whole thing, [the miracle] of organization.

David: There's the stated requirements and then there's the ones that the morons who invent the operation never get around to thinking of but expect you to take care of anyway. We got Noah his wife, his three sons and their wives - we got eight. So you've got to supply for eight people and all these animals. But then if you're going to be a literalist and read the chapters before this, then wait a minute! There's more than just eight. It says here that Methuselah lived to be 969 years old; if he lives to be 969, he's got to be on the ark, because it happens before he's dead. But they don't mention him, but you've got to feed him!

Jack: Either that or he's drowned.

David: No, he can't live to be 969 and drown. That's the point. His age span is given there, if you're a literalist. This means he has to be there, hiding in this little room in a corner someplace - hiding out - they don't want to talk about him. He's kind of a grouchy old coot.

Alan: So planning an operation like this always has its consequences.

David: Yeah.

Alan: Now all of us were involved in operations of one kind or another that involved planning and supply, so in our experience of war, and being aware of how difficult it was just looking at this, of how difficult it was to provide supplies, did any of us have the supplies we needed? The physical supplies?

David: Usually the wrong ones!

Russ: Well, in addition, my friend was the chaplain at the depot in Danang; it was an utter nightmare. And I've read, plus being at Command and Staff College courses, where we got all this stuff over there and then during the draw-down what in the world were we to do with it? Well, we left it, a lot of it.

Alan: Buried it.

David: Property disposal. And they had a great, big compactor.

Russ: So your point is well taken, Alan. This was a mammoth, mammoth undertaking logistically for G-4.

Alan: G-4.

Russ: Could it be "J-4?"

Harvey: "J-4" What do you mean?

Alan: "Jehovah-4!"

Harvey: Oh, geez!

Alan: O.K. Did you have the stuff you needed materially? Did the system work?

Charlie: I remember the rumor started out that one of our companies was out in a defensive position and they didn't have any trip flares. I got in the rumor mill; I told all the supply sergeants on the pad that story, and it even got to the general. That evening there was a pyramid of trip flares laying on the pad of the stuff that all of our friends - including the general - had "appropriated" for this unit that was out in this exposed position. So it didn't work the way it was supposed to. I guess the answer is, "no."

David: I had to go to Saigon once to talk to the people higher up the line about supplies. So I went and talked to the clerks that got those little requisitions and I saw these three guys with their desks piled high and sweating like crazy, and this other fellow going like this, not doing much, and I said to him, "Who are you?" And he said, "I handle priority 4. Nobody even sends anything priority 4; it's always priority 1 or 2." Guess where all mine went after that - priority 4! I got everything right away.

Russ: There's a story about communion wine. They ordered it by the gross, so instead of getting 144 bottles, they got 144 cases - God awful thing - you'd have to take communion every hour on the hour to get rid of it!

Jack: So that's the secret of your success.

Linda: You say that as if it were a problem.

Charlie: Ever drink that much Angelica?

Alan: Did you get there with stuff you didn't need?

Charlie: Oh yeah.

Alan: What stuff didn't you need?

Charlie: My temperate weather clothing that they made me bring.

Ken: It went into a Conex container at the base camp and you got it out when you left after a year.

Ray: We received shipments that, somehow, when the stenciling was put on the containers, was stuff that should have gone to Korea and came to Vietnam.

David: Long underwear?

Ray. Long underwear, field jacket liners, all this stuff that in

120 degrees you sure as hell don't want to put on. The other issue is, as was mentioned, all of the disposal. And having been in Long Binh and having walked into unguarded nuclear weapons bunkers and bunkers containing nerve gas, what the hell happened to all that shit? In whose hands is it now? But - coming out of S-4 - being a munitions specialist, being out in the field as well as the base camp, one of the major issues we faced, and this especially was true in the Delta, was - somebody would call "We need fresh water out here." And the damn helicopters wouldn't get off the ground because the air was so damp they could barely pick themselves up - let alone the supplies. You know, you think the people - and we're talking pure drinking water - who are in desperate need - because of the temperature, because of the sweat that they're putting out - to replenish what is essential to life, and yet it couldn't get there.

Alan: Ken, you were saying that you put your stuff that you didn't need in a Conex box? Or put it in storage?

Ken: Yes. Back as base camp in Bear Cat.

Alan Did any of the rest of you find that you had stuff that you didn't need? - Everybody [here] had stuff that they didn't need when we got there. Extra uniforms. I remember being in the navy and being newly commissioned as an Ensign, they told us we should always be with all of our uniforms; we should take everything with us.

Ken: Oh my!

Alan: Oh my, yeah! So I had a set of blues.

David: I sold mine before I went over.

Jack: I had a set of greens and khaki short sleeved uniforms the army still had at that point, and it all went into a suitcase at base camp and I went to that suitcase - and civilian clothes - when I went out of the area for R&R or when I left. But that was the only times that suitcase had any relevance to me; otherwise it was there, but of no use.

Alan: So you had to make choices about what you would keep and what you would get rid of

Ken: Yeah.

Alan: And choices about other kinds of stuff you would "appropriate?" Anybody do any "appropriation?"

Linda: Let the record show that a lot of hands went into the air on that one!

David: I refuse to answer question on the grounds that I was in the quartermaster corps, and I don't answer questions like that!

Ken: We did a lot of midnight requisitioning, or we bartered.

Alan: Midnight requisitioning or bartering?

Ken: We bartered with the navy a lot.

Russ: Sometimes people got caught. I knew a man whose name I will not mention who was preparing to go to the chief's office - bird colonel - and because of some things he did on logistics - a high level congressman's wife seemed to have that information - he didn't get that appointment.

David: We were a bastard organization of civilians and military, of course. So I had a civilian who was supposedly up above me somewhere in the chain of command and he had been a career navy enlisted - long, long years - had first come to Vietnam way back - so he had years of being over there - and he had all kinds of deals going - we just never could quite nail him for it - but I started looking in my records and kept finding things that I had put in there disappeared and finally traced one of them and he had it and had changed it. Well, anyway, I finally had enough to tell the local commander, who was a major, what was going on and then it was out of my hands. I found I couldn't do anything more about it. Instead of the guy taking a trip to jail, he was transferred to Korea. I guess they just looked out for each other at that level. He was selling it downtown, went downtown in Qui Nhon and was selling the stuff.

Alan: So for all this physical stuff - you made choices about what you kept and what you didn't keep. You appropriated what you needed in the course of the conflict. What about when you arrived in Vietnam - how spiritually and mentally prepared were you? And did you choose what to keep and what to throw away? And did you appropriate what you needed? What was it you needed?

Ken: Physically - I'm on a different level - I was thinking physically it took a while to figure out what you didn't need. I guess spiritually and professionally, in a sense, as a chaplain a lot of practices went out the window and new ones arrived. A lot of types of prayer, what you prayed about, how you prayed.

Alan: What went out the window? From the chaplain's point of view?

Ken: Formulas - rituals, regulations, style of preaching. Some traditional, I wouldn't say, morality, but certainly moral understandings.

Russ: One acquisition for me was ecumenicity, or the beginnings of it. An increase in whatever level I had achieved at that point; I don't remember what that was. But this exposure gave me a new understanding of the wide range of humanity.

John: I have a question for the chaplains who were there. Were you given kind of stock answers?

Ken: By whom?

John: From above, that you were supposed to say.

Ken: I don't think so.

Charlie: I don't think so.

Ken: No, I think in a lot of ways we were left alone by the brass. The medics weren't. We rarely saw the JAG. These are the three branches that you want. And we rarely saw the JAG. The medics weren't left alone, but they just did their job and in a sense I guess we did too. But the only time that I had relationships with big brass was when there had been a problem. And I wrote something; then I would get asked about it.

Charlie: A chaplain wrote to a layman in our church about the moral conditions in his operation. The layperson's name was Lyndon Baines Johnson. He got noticed!

Russ: There were chaplains who were in adversarial relationships with their commanders because they took moral positions.

Alan: What happened to a chaplain that took a moral position?

Russ: They got moved, or somehow they appealed over the heads to the next higher headquarters and had someone to take their side. So there was a variety of things people could do.

Alan: Again - to you chaplain types - Ken has said that you had to suspend certain sorts of moral understandings?

Ken: Not suspend so much, but it all got changed, all

different shadows to it.

Linda: Textures?

Ken: "Thou shalt not kill." How do you talk to a kid who just came in from an operation and he just blew five people away? He wants to talk to you about it and he's moving towards the whole idea that he just will not do that again. And he won't go out. So what do you do with him? You see, the only way you got out of the field, at least in some ways, was to get yourself certified by the psych, or you pleaded conscientious objection now because of your combat experience. Because of what happened to you, and the commanders did not like their troops pleading conscientious objection.

Charlie: You must have had a tough outfit because if we had a combat veteran that that happened to, we put him in supply. All of our supply clerks and even our platoon leaders were all guys who had had the course - because we had that much trust between the doctor and the chaplain and the colonel.

Russ: But this is just one more example - Ken telling one set of circumstances - you're telling a different set - so it's a whole variety of responses.

Jack: It's interesting - even chaplain-to-chaplain - we've got four chaplains here and we have four different wars. Because I'm sitting here thinking, "Well, they were in their war, and I was in mine."

Charlie: The elephant. The Asian elephant.

Jack: Yeah. In some respects mine was fortunate. I was thinking did I have any occasion when I needed to take a moral stand or something, and if I did, I've completely blocked it out because there's no memory of it. But for the Fourth operating in the Central Highlands, the opportunity to damage civilians was much less than it was in some of the more populated areas.

Charlie: We fraternized with the monkeys.

Jack: We mostly dealt with enemy soldiers and generals.

Charlie: The NVA regulars.

Jack: Going back to your earlier question. What did we wear, and what did we leave behind? There's an interesting analogy that suddenly struck me that, from my experience, what I really needed that year as a chaplain was kind of spiritual jungle fatigues -- whatever they were -- and I think I spent the whole year in class "A's." At this point, I can say I wish I had the jungle fatigues, but I couldn't tell you specifically enough what the spiritual jungle fatigues would consist of so that I could pick them out of the supply room on the next trip back to Vietnam. I'm not sure what they are, but I didn't have then, and I wish I had.

Russ: My earlier trip to Korea probably was much more excruciatingly traumatic to me than was Vietnam, because that's where I did a lot of my work. If I had not discovered the grace of God in Korea, I would have lost not only my faith but my mind, because I saw people falling like moral flies, or morally falling like flies. At least, in the way that I looked at morality and I really had to come to grips with that. And that was when I did it; it was in Korea, which was '64-'65.

Alan: For the rest of us that weren't chaplain types and did not have the great preparation that the chaplains had . . .

Jack: Huh?

Alan: Let it be shown that all the chaplains laughed at that point . . . How prepared were you all? What kind of things did you acquire to keep yourselves spiritually and mentally whole, or did you not acquire anything, or did you fall apart?

Linda: I just know that everything that I had believed to be true - duty, God, country - if you do the right thing, everything will work out fine - If you work hard, you'll be rewarded - everything that I believed in was taken away. And I don't recall that I had anything with which to replace it. So basically I filled that gap with booze. And it took probably took me about twenty-five or thirty years after the fact to find something to fill that hole.

Russ: One thing, by contrast, chaplains, at least for myself, were fifteen years older than a lot of enlisted men. How old were you when you were there.

Linda: I was older than most; I was twenty years old.

Russ: O.K. The difference between twenty and forty would make a lot of difference.

Linda: I turned twenty-one while I was there; boy, that was a party!

Russ: You know, I have compassion for them. Women filled themselves with booze. Men filled themselves with sex and booze when they felt empty. Chaplains may not have done it quite so much.

Linda: You know, I think I threw myself into my job too. I became very intense about my work.

Ray: I think one of the things - and this really came out of my reading the book by Tim O'Brien, "If I Die . . ." - his conversation with the base chaplain who was sort of the go-between between where he was and the C.O. And reading that it sparked a memory within me of during our time - I said we went over as a unit - we all went on this ship that was called the USS Upshor which we referred to as the USS "Rupture" - because the damn thing had sunk twice before - you could walk by the gunwale plates and kick them and big chunks would fly out.

Harvey: You're a strong man. Less strong men may not have done that damage.

Ray: That's beside the point. I went to the chaplain on the ship with some serious questions about life and death and the issues of "thou shalt not kill" and all of that. The next thing I knew I got a phone call from my C.O. wanting to know whit in the hell right I had going to the chaplain talking about these things! And I mean he stated back almost verbatim everything that I had said to the chaplain. And so I had a very big block, never spoke to another chaplain while I was there.

Ken: I wouldn't of.

David: Confidentiality?

Ray: Went right out the window.

Jack: If you put that guy's name out on the table his life's in danger.

Ray: I wish I could remember his name; maybe that's a mental block. I don't know. But that was my experience.

Alan: The passage that we looking at in Genesis - the story of Noah - talks about really an apocalypse, the end of everything that breathes upon the earth except for those things that are floating and safe within the ark. It sort of brings to mind that old story about having to destroy the village in order to save it. It talks about the water covering the face of the earth. Sort of a long monsoon. Do you resonate in any way with that image of apocalypse? Did you witness anything that you might call apocalyptic that gave you the feeling that you were somewhere in the midst of a breakdown of everything? Linda has said that everything that she took there in the way of God, duty, country - all of hat went to pieces. Now I can identify with that because everything that they told me in the training before I went in country, the minute I got there, it all went out the door. Everything that they told me at the briefings in Saigon at MACV had no relationship to reality when I arrived in Danang.

Linda: Yeah.

Alan: I didn't realize I had to go so little distance to go into a different country, as from Saigon MACV to the field in Danang.

John: The rules were always changing, and/or there weren't any.

Alan: Is that what apocalypse is? When the rules break down? When the rites and rituals done work anymore?

John: It certainly added to the feeling of unsafety!

Ken: Even in - I was in the "river rats" - the mobile riverine force - we had a ways of doing things. Tet blew it to pieces and that kind of combat - that was apocalyptic. There was no more even giving combat orders - it was survival.

Alan: Just like Noah floating on the ark, you have to survive somehow.

Ken: Yeah. It was totally different. That was physical; you didn't know which end was up.

Ray: I also think that sort of an apocalyptic shock was going from an area that was a free fire zone to an area that you had to get permission. Prove it was the enemy; prove they had a weapon . . . and an intent.

David: Sort of like the major in our compound one night - what he was doing there . . . he wasn't one of ours - but we were firing back. Another one of those things where they were attacking the induction center across the road and kind of missing a lot and coming our way. We were firing and he said, "Did you call QUINTOC [Qui Nhon Tactical Operation Center] for permission to fire back?' And the sergeant next to me said, "Shut up and feed that belt!" And he did. Something went zinging by him at that moment so . . . Yeah. But I had to live with that all the time except when I was in the pass. That was weird that this was a war but you couldn't fire back unless someone told you "O.K. I guess it's O.K. now. We'll think about it. We'll get back to you in the morning."

Jack: Interesting thought. But I'm not exactly sure how it fits in to all this but the - if this story of Noah and the ark were a dream and were being analyzed on kind of a gestalt basis, then we, the dreamers, would be identifying as pieces of ourselves all the elements in this dream. We are Noah; we are the ark; we are the flood. I was really just sitting here getting into that picture - not the picture of us as being there and the flood washing over us - which is also true - but the picture of us being the flood destroying everything in our path, inundating everything that we touched, changing everything that we touched.

Alan: I know that in Danang the Americans just sort of flooded in there and occupied the Tien Sha peninsula so the people that had been out there - the Vietnamese - were just dispossessed into the shacks along the road.

Jack: Of course, they knew that we were there to save them, and they appreciated this, and none of them became VC as a result.

Linda: There's another apocalyptic moment: lies become truth, or truth becomes lies.

Ken: The topsy-turviness of business as usual over there. I found when I came home that it took me a while to accustomize myself – that "that" wasn't' what the world was. Home was like . . . home was a dream . . . home was not normal. That "that" had become normal.

Linda: "That" was more real somehow.

Russ: Let me . . . my experience of life is . . . but I was not exposed to combat when I was over there. And when I was with Ken, though I didn't know it at the time, he had already had one tour and the experience that he had and what he talks about -- I had to come to this conference to know what Vietnam was about; in other words, that was how little I was exposed to the war. But there were a fair number of people that were rear-echelon . . .

Linda: REMF's [*very common abbreviation meaning "rear-echelon mother fuckers"*]

Russ: There was a whole host of people who were there who didn't know anything about Vietnam.

Jack: Of course, we had to come here to hear about you driving through the An Khe pass singing Gospel hymns!

Russ: I was a REMF really.

David: You didn't know they were shooting at you up there in that place?

Russ: No. No.

Jack: He just thought they didn't like his singing!

David: That's it.

Harvey: And in Texas that's how they demonstrated it.

Jack: He thought he was back home.

Charlie: How do we know that it was the Vietnamese that were shooting at his singing?

Russ: That adds to the confusion; there were some people that had no awareness that a flood was going on.

Alan: In the passage from Genesis it says that everybody that was on firm ground died. So somewhere you had to learn how to survive not on firm ground; some people called it quicksand, the big muddy . . .

John: Slippery slope. . .

Alan: The slippery slope. Survival was a matter of having no firm ground and being able to deal with that. Whether it was from physical supplies where you get what you get, or whether it was mentally or spiritually you had to learn how to tread water, or tread mud.

Charlie: It was really slippery during the monsoon.

John: It makes me wonder about what could we depend on over there? A lot of times it felt to me as if the only thing I could depend on was chaos.

Ken: I'm sorry. Was what?

David: Chaos. It's about the same as Laos, only not pronounced like it. With a "CH"

Charlie: How would you put that in military terminology?

Linda: SNAFU -- situation normal . . .

Charlie: "Don't mean nothin'"

Alan: Go back to what you were saying, John. Say it again slowly.

John: The only thing that I felt I could depend on was chaos.

Alan: O.K. The only thing that I felt I could depend on when I was there was myself, because my experience in 71-72 was that there was no chain of command. I mean when I got there in Danang – first of all, they didn't expect me and about the first thing the commander said to me was, "What the hell am I supposed to do with you?" Then I just ended up doing whatever little odd jobs needed to be done - some very strange kinds of things - and they were exciting - but people were leaving so fast that I decided that the only thing that I could really depend upon was myself.

John: And the trouble I see with that was that I saw a lot of guys, who I thought had their shit together, that depended on themselves, and did everything right, and still got killed.

Alan: I want to call your attention to the end of the story a little bit, and the floodwaters retreat and then, as I read this thing, Noah does a few things right away. He had survived the terrible apocalyptic flood; he immediately does three things. First thing he does after coming off the ark is offer up blood sacrifices of the fruits of the pure animals and pure fowl. The second thing he does is he plants a vineyard and gets drunk. Everybody's waving hands now . . . O.K.

Linda: And then he's stripped naked. I think I mentioned that.

Alan: Well, he plants a vineyard and gets drunk; and the third thing that he does - he curses his son.

Charlie: The one that saw him naked.

Alan: Yes. The one that uncovered his nakedness.

Jack: And God looked down and said, "I sure made a good choice."

Alan: The question that I propose: have we, out of our experience, somehow seen the nakedness of the father, the parent, and been cursed because of it?

Charlie: Yes - and people don't want to hear it.

Alan: Don't want to hear what?

Charlie: That daddy's naked. They want to hear it, but they don't want to hear it!

Alan: Looking back, what did that nakedness uncover . . . what did we see?

Charlie: Our flaws - warts and all

Alan: What flaws?

Jack: Our father's flaws.

Alan: What were the flaws of the father?

Jack: Dishonesty.

David: Politicians and thieves.

Charlie: Cowardice.

Jack: Avarice.

Alan: And how did you see that? As you looked at, even uncovered, that nakedness, what did it look like? What are some examples of that nakedness?

Russ: McNamara's book. Of course, that's well after the fact. But I sure saw some nakedness there.

Alan: Nakedness as?

Russ: Dishonesty. "Oh, this was a mistake." And I think, "You're a numbers man; you're a genius; you're a whiz kid. Yet, 58,000 people and you pass it off as a mistake?"

Linda: Of course, it was more than that. The lies that went . . . we talked about this last night . . . the reporting lies . . . the discrepancies about what was really going on versus what was being reported. You know, that deception.

John: How about greed?

Alan: Greed?

Russ: Yes. Lady Bird Johnson. I never saw . . .

David: Yes.

Russ: When I was in Danang I saw this fleet of SeaVan pass us on the other side of Marble Mountain - row after row of these vans - and then on Route 1, there they were again coming out of Danang, and then the building . . .

Ken: MRK

Linda: You're talking about the contractors.

Ken: But who owned them?

Jack: Lady Bird had a big share in the contractors.

Ken: That was the rumor.

Ray: I think one of the nakedest pieces that I encountered was having to report to . . . the office which I was reporting back to in relationship to experimental warheads, and so on. That we were using - some of which I called into question because of their "No, they had not signed the Geneva Convention and therefore they were outside" and we could use whatever the hell we wanted to on them. There was the closeness I had to a particular clerk who showed me a photo-static copy of a note that simply said across the top "From the desk of LBJ." One of those very common little notepads - and it was sent in a way that would not be through channels, through all of the stuff - but this clerk had taken the opportunity to make a photo-static copy - that old photo-static machine - that simply said, "Westy, you can tell our good old boys that the reason we are there is to show the god damn Russians we can kick somebody's god damn ass. LBJ" And the presumption on the clerk's part was that all the FNG's coming in telling us what was going on stateside - how was he to balance this out? This was just before Abrams took over. How was he supposed to balance out that these two groups of diverse people - one who went in without the knowledge of all the protesting, all of the other stuff - and then the others - so he gets this note to tell them that they're there to kick somebody's god damn ass to prove to the Russians we can. I think that changed a lot of my attitude about why I was there.

David: I'd gone to school in Berkeley, and I saw plenty of the protest stuff going on in 69-70 - with Cambodia - I happened to be on leave from Fort Irwin in the Mojave Desert and I went up to see some friends in Berkeley - I joined them - heck, I didn't want to go there! And then I went back to Fort Irwin. And went to Vietnam right after. But I'd seen it here, but somehow it didn't affect me the same way as when I got over there and saw the divisions amongst people around base camps. Now my wife's cousin who was in the 173rd and I went up and saw him when they were out at the edge of what they were calling Fire Base Buffalo which they turned the Fourth Division's place into at An Khe with a smaller perimeter. And his squad was about half black, half white. They seemed to be getting along fine there, but he said to me, "You ought to see us when we stand down. These guys and us never talk." And everywhere I went that was anything near like a base camp, an airbase, anywhere away from that situation, the blacks are here, the whites are here, and all the secret handshakes are going on - and just a sense of how divided we were. I was telling myself, this country is coming apart at the seams - I don't think it's going to stay together. If I go home, will there be home there to go to? If I make it to go home, will there be a place to go to? It was frightening.

Russ: Alan, did you bring up the Christmas bombing in an earlier conversation?

Ken: I did.

Russ: O.K. To me, that was much later in the war - 1972 . . .

Alan: Say something about what it brought up. Tell me what did it do to you?

Russ: Well, it was well after the fact, you know, when I really began to become aware of this; that we're saying "peace, peace" while there is no peace. And we're cultivating war directly from the White House - this memo - with utter dishonesty - this worldwide, global dishonesty.

Jack: In a sense it almost transcends dishonesty. In that note, yes, this note if it was written as a private note - it was a private note but it wasn't written as a secret note. He was telling Westmoreland, and if Westmoreland had gotten on Armed Force radio and read exactly what Lyndon Johnson said in that that note, he would have been carrying out the instructions of the note, even if it was intended to be non-public. Part of the nakedness to me of Lyndon Johnson is that he had no concept that kind of thought was something to be ashamed of. No concept. Like the emperor's new clothes, he thought he was wearing clothes when he was standing out there buck-naked.

Alan: Good point. So we come back, having seen the nakedness of the father and end up being cursed. Cursed in what way? What does it feel like to be cursed?

David: *Sig heil!*

Ken: Not welcomed home.

Linda: I was referred to as "There goes one of Uncle Sam's whores."

Ray: To return after Hawaii, to be believed to have been a deserter when I could document having been in the hospital for that entire period of time.

Alan: Then returned back to Vietnam.

John: I think at some level too the sanction for killing was revoked.

Linda: Yeah.

John: Upon our return, you know, if you were called baby-killers or any other despicable names, worse than dirt, you can begin to feel that all of these things you did for our country, under the guise of duty, honor, and responsibility, including maybe murder - killing in a war is supposed to be killing in a war, but if you don't have the sanction from your country, what is it?

Linda: First degree.

Alan: Lost the sanction. How have you lived with the curse?

Ray: Not well.

Charlie: Yeah.

Ken: You cope. You cope, and every once and a while, you crash.

Alan: And what happens after you crash? Pick up or just stay down? Is that the choice?

Ken: I guess, at least, in my own case I picked up, with help. This group helps. Ten years ago, that was the first time I think I faced a lot of it. In Washington, first time around.

Linda: You pick up and cope again and you find others who are coping and get some sense of connection. It doesn't make it any easier per se - but somehow it does - not being quite alone in your coping.

Charlie: If you can get over that trying to regain what you lost, it helps. For me, when I try to say I'm going to get the magic pill or bullet and I going to . . . that a trap, that's a dead trap for me.

Linda: It's like I said, I think I finally got to the point where I realized I was never going to be O.K. And it's O.K.

Alan: And the Scripture says - "The people that were on firm ground died." So we're still surviving - with no firm ground.

Darkness and Dreams

Excerpts from Genesis 28 and 32 (NRSV)

Jacob left Beer-sheba and went toward Haran. He came to a certain place and stayed there for the night, because the sun had set. Taking one of the stones of the place, he put it under his head and lay down in that place. And he dreamed that there was a ladder set up on the earth, the top of it reaching to heaven; and the angels of God were ascending and descending on it. And the Lord stood beside him and said, "I am the Lord, the God of Abraham your father and the God of Isaac; the land on which you lie I will give to you and to your offspring; and your offspring shall be like the dust of the earth, and you shall spread abroad to the west and to the east and to the north and to the south; and all the families of the earth shall be blessed in you and in your offspring. Know that I am with you and will keep you wherever you go, and will bring you back to this land; for I will not leave you until I have done what I have promised you." Then Jacob woke from his sleep and said, "Surely the Lord is in this place—and I did not know it!" And he was afraid, and said, "How awesome is this place! This is none other than the house of God, and this is the gate of heaven." So Jacob rose early in the morning, and he took the stone that he had put under his head and set it up for a pillar and poured oil on the top of it. He called that place Bethel;

Then Jacob made a vow, saying, "If God will be with me, and will keep me in this way that I go, and will give me bread to eat and clothing to wear, so that I come again to my father's house in peace, then the Lord shall be my God, and this stone, which I have set up for a pillar, shall be God's house; and of all that you give me I will surely give one-tenth to you."

The same night he got up and took his two wives, his two maids, and his eleven children, and crossed the ford of the Jabbok. He took them and sent them across the stream, and likewise everything that he had. Jacob was left alone; and a man wrestled with him until daybreak. When the man saw that he did not prevail against Jacob, he struck him on the hip socket; and Jacob's hip was put out of joint as he wrestled with him. Then he said, "Let me go, for the day is breaking." But Jacob said, "I will not let you go, unless you bless me." So he said to him, "What is your name?" And he said, "Jacob." Then the man said, "You shall no longer be called Jacob (Heel-Sneak), but Israel (God-fighter), for you have striven with God and with humans, and have prevailed." Then Jacob asked him, "Please tell me your name." But he said, "Why is it that you ask my name?" And there he blessed him. So Jacob called the place Peniel, saying, "For I have seen God face to face, and yet my life is preserved." The sun rose upon him as he passed Penuel, limping because of his hip.

* * * * *

Participating: Alan, Charlie, David, Ray, Jack, Jeff, John, Ken, Linda, Russ

* * * * *

Alan: We're all familiar with the character of Jacob – a rather dubious character in the Bible – one who was well known as a trickster, a person of duplicity, a cheat, a deceiver, and having said all of these things about him, let me ask who among us identifies with Jacob? Other then me. You all do?

Russ: *Mea culpa.*

Alan: *Mea culpa.* And why do you feel so overcome as to identify with Jacob, Russ?

Russ: Deceptions are responsible. I keep them from myself a lot of the time, but I occasionally get an inkling from myself that I have been tricky.

David: Jacob sleeps in church. In the Sanctuary. That's what I tell people when they sleep through sermons. "Well, it's an old custom. If you too see visions of angels descending, that's great."

Russ: Why don't you tell them they're asleep in Jesus?

David: I could do that. Truly, as an anthropologist, it was a custom then to sleep in a place known to be a religious sanctuary hoping to have a vision from whoever the deity of the area was, so he was following actually good religious practice, believe it or not.

Alan: I'm just sitting here thinking about the various places I've fallen asleep and which places might be considered sacred places, and which places where we might have had visions of angels ascending and descending. Have you ever run across an angel?

Harvey: You mean other than my daughter?

Charlie: Don't know.

Alan: Were there people that we met, we served with that were considered angels? Certainly the nurses.

John: Medics.

David: Chopper pilots.

Linda: Ascending and descending!

John: Whoever brought the mail.

David: That's for sure.

Jack: Unless it was a "Dear John."

John: Well, every one of mine was!

Ken: Angel means messenger.

Russ: So mailman fits.

Alan: Did you receive messengers in country? Linda, you were in communications; you dealt with messengers all the time. Did you ascribe to them any angelic qualities?

Linda: No, most of the messages were not necessarily good news.

John: Well, being able to send or receive messages on the radio to get some ammunition or call in fire was certainly angelic!

David: Of course, this messenger wounded Jacob.

Alan: Ah, eventually. Say some more about messengers and wounding. Anybody got any thoughts on that?

David: The tape I got from my wife where she told me, "I can tell you now but we were in an accident last week. The car is totaled; we're O.K., sort of." Or another tape I got from her; I was listening and she was sitting there watching the news and talking to the tape and she said, "Oh my God. I'm so scared. They just blew up the ammunition dump at Qui Nhon. I hope you're alive."

Charlie: Again?

David: Well, this was the first time. Until then I hadn't really thought . . . it happened. It was irritating. It was . . . I guess I was numb enough by then I really didn't feel scared when it started blowing. But when I got the tape I was scared because I heard how frightened she was.

Alan: And she had gotten a message of great fright, a message that held a possibility of changing her life, and to you in country it was, "Eh. There goes another ammo dump!"

Harvey: But it was painful to Dave to hear her terror.

David: How scared she was!

Ray: Once I was sharing with Jeff – one of the times we were out inhaling the toxins – my mother had always said, in relationship to the period of time in which my father served overseas in World War Two, that she always waited for that message, "I am safe; I am alive." And my father never understood that until I was the one who was leaving and now he was at home sweating the proverbial bullets until he heard, or they heard, from me. And weeks might go by and I might get a letter but would be unable to respond to it because of location or whatever. And on one particular occasion getting the message and then trying to get back to base to use one of the MACV phones, you know, where you could call – "Hello, this is Ray, Over." All that bullshit that you had to go through . . .

David: The MARS radio.

Ray: MARS . . . yeah. When I got the letter about the death of my grandfather. Now I did not look at the date of the letter. I was simply receiving a message – you might say it's the message of the angel of death. My grandfather had died, whom I had been so close to but was so distant from. And a desire to somehow find a way home to attend his service which was already two weeks behind; and that strange sense, that feeling as though a big piece of your life has just been taken from you – regardless of what was happening in country – and it was enough so that it distracted me to the point where this friend of mine had just gotten back from Hawaii – I don't know why he got to go. He wasn't married. It was just one of those strange things that happened; it just happened that he got one of the Hawaiian R&R's. He came back – after stopping at Guam – we all know – you could purchase up to one US wine gallon and he drank two fifths of the one US wine gallon in Hawaii and brought three back with him, and we sat out on the running board of a deuce and a half on fire watch – which to anybody else you mention "fire watch" and anybody would say, "Why were you sitting up watching for a fire?" It just goes right over their head. We sat there and started off with a bottle of Southern Comfort, the most god-awful stuff in the world, and we drank that sucker dry – right out of the bottle. He then went and got a bottle of Smirnoff's 100 proof vodka and by that time it didn't make any difference and we drank that sucker dry – and then I woke up who I thought was the next person to be on fire watch, and we were sleeping in tents and all around our tent – because we had various things from S-4 that needed to be "protected " - there was razor wire. And the tent was laid over a wooden frame and my bunk was smack dab in the middle with 2 2x4's nailed together over it. And we, during the course of that night, came under fire, under a rocket attack, and the tent that we were in took a direct hit from a 122, and the next thing I remember was somebody hollering my name, "Blitzfelt! Where are you?" They had all heard the sirens; but I was so blotto that I didn't hear the 122 mm rockets exploding. And I walked out - I gently freed myself from that wire -- and literally did not have a scratch on me. And I don't know whether you call that some form of miracle or not, but I don't know why in the hell I'm still here given the fact that the bursting radius of 122 is about 1500 meters and I've seen pieces of shrapnel from 122's just cleave a tree right in two! But there I was – no tent – nothing left except this totally naked individual – lying in the razor wire with these voices coming from the bunker that was at the end of the tent. "Blitzfelt! Where are you?" I mean I don't know what to do with that. Is that "that guardian angel?" Or a supposed block, or whatever you call it - I don't know . . .

Alan: Would any of you chaplains like to deal with that?

David: Didn't they give you that list of things to say?

Ken: It's in my room.

Charlie: I think that it's in the same place with the little Vietnamese lady that's pacing off the camp all the time. Asleep in a sapper attack!

Russ: What did you do your CPE in? What do you think?

John: What does that make you feel?

David: How do you feel about it?

Ray: I feel like one lucky shit! The other piece of it is that 4x4 - the two 2x4's nailed together – was right smack dab . . . my cot hit the post right in the middle and the post was gone. Did I go through it? Or did I go around it?

Charlie: Or did you go over it?

Harvey: Or under it.

Charlie: I vote for over.

Ken: Two men will be in a field; one will be taken and one will not.

David: It's like the guy next to me. I was at the MARS station and we started hearing the buzz and then the whole room started to vibrate – it was a rocket coming in – and so we headed for their little half a culvert pipe thing with the sand bags over it. We got in there and after everything quit blowing for a while somebody said, "Everybody O.K." And everyone's going, "yeah, yeah." And the guy next to me said, "Except I got a bunch of shrapnel in my arm." Now my arm was there, and there was nothing in it, but his arm was bleeding like crazy. So, one will be taken. another missed.

Jack: I think one of the things that this chaplain might have said in a situation like that is that, "With respect to why you got saved and somebody else didn't, I'm not sure I want to go there. I don't want to touch that. But what is incumbent is, now that you're here, and in a sense have no right to be, then that kind of lays on you the task to make something out of it." And that's really probably why we all are sitting around the table. I mean if you hear everybody's story then who has a right to be here?

Ray: And I think that part of the guilt associated with survival.

Charlie: It makes no sense.

Jack: It's interesting – if you look back at some of the stories of great lives of one sort or another, often there is this element of making or finding some kind of meaning in what otherwise might be looked on as a chance event. I mean, you look at the founding father of our denomination, John Wesley. One of his big things was that there was a fire in the rectory when he was a kid, and he always thought of himself as "a brand plucked from the burning."

Ken: Ray, maybe you couldn't give a reason for the fact that you survived, but your daughter who used to jump in your arms can give you a great reason.

Ray: The other piece about this story that strikes me is the ladder and the story of the angels ascending and descending. And the story that caused great humility in which the young minister died and went to heaven and St. Peter met him and said, "Here's a piece of chalk. There's a chalkboard. Go start writing your sins upon that board." And he said, "I was a minister. I didn't sin." And he said, "Wait a minute. Do you remember that twenty-five cents your mother gave you to put in the collection plate and instead of doing it, you went out and bought an ice cream on the way home?" "Well, that . . ." "Write it down!" And there was a ladder beside the board, and as he started writing his sins down he'd take a step or two up the ladder to get a little higher on the board; and as he got higher he saw a pair of feet coming down. And so he moved to one side and the other figure came down the other side. He noticed it was his bishop. He said, "Bishop, what are you doing?" The Bishop replied, "Why, I'm going to get another piece of chalk!" Ascending and descending.

David: Annual Conference is where you tell that?

Ray: I've told that from the pulpit. It was told at Annual Conference by a bishop.

Harvey: To the extent that an angel is a messenger rather than the anthropomorphic, supernatural entity with wings that we often think of, then I – as someone who was not there but who needs to get the message – I mean because I need to get the message – which makes all of you angels, in the sense that you are messengers. Here's Jacob, kind of a delinquent, shady guy – kind of ordinary – but he is what he is – and in the middle of the night, the messenger come to wrestle him and change him and whacks him in the hip – just to make sure when he wakes up and he remembers it really happened; and I think that in my brief but intense association with this organization I'm constantly struggling with trying to understand and absorb and honor the message; that is the perspective that I, as someone who seeks to receive the message on behalf of those who didn't go, bring. I think the people who didn't go, who didn't have this experience, need this message and I have this instinct, this deep intuition, and I'm acting upon it and we were just speaking before the session started and Russ said, "It's not over. Vietnam's not over." And I share that view. I support that view. It's not over because I don't think that the message or messages have been received yet. And maybe it did take thirty years. In an interesting way I feel particularly close to Ray because this is our first year here and after about thirty years roughly it really seems to have hit you hard – a number of events may have triggered it so there's something about you and I being on the same time maybe – we're on a similar schedule. I see you folks as messengers; it's unmistakable.

Russ: I'd like to piggyback on that. Because you have complained when I have said that I wasn't in combat. Ten years ago I had this same sense – and I've never lost that sense – this group of people who were exposed to combat in Vietnam, which I was not while I was there – they were messengers to me. Twenty years after the fact. I'm eternally grateful. It almost brings tears to my eyes to think of the message that has been brought to me, and God has granted me the power to hear. It's kind of in my soul; what do I do with this message now that I've got it?

Harvey: I have the same problem. Or perhaps problem is a bad word. I have the same blessing – you and I share the same blessing. That's why when we introduced ourselves on Monday night I thought about it and I said, "My surprise is exceeded only by my gratitude." And a roomful of strangers looked at me and thought, "What the heck is he talking about?" Now you know what the heck "he's" talking about, but I share a blessing with Russ, a very strong sense of that. One thought, Alan, for consideration is as we move on is whether the role of the messenger, the role of the angel, is a healing one? If you are messengers, is that a helpful perspective? Is that healing?

Russ: Well now, the angel hit him, and so he wounded him. So he not only brought a message, but he also brought a wound, and you can't listen to these stories without finding yourself wounded.

Jack: An angel brought Jacob a wound; he brought Jacob a new name; and thereby he brought Jacob a new mission.

Linda: He brought him a blessing too.

Jack: Was that separate or was that part of these three? The blessing was the name, wasn't it? The mission. Henceforth – and the name is his character. The re-naming is a re-characterization. He is no longer – I love this – Heel-Sneak – no longer are you Heel-Sneak, but instead of this you are God-Fighter. Now there's a title of a book for the popular audience. From "Con-Fighter to God-Fighter."

Russ: Well, it says that near the end he gives him a farewell blessing, but it doesn't say what it was; so it is there.

Jack: O.K. You're seeing the blessing as something different; I see the blessing as the re-naming. But you're right, then there's a farewell blessing. But the reason I saw the re-naming as a blessing was that right there in the midst of the struggle when Jacob still has his hands on the angel, and the angel says, "Day's come up. Let me go." And Jacob says, "No, I'm not going to let you go until you bless me." And then the angel says, "O.K. What is your name?" Jacob tells him and the angels say, "O.K. Good. Henceforth it won't be Heel-Sneak, it will be God-Fighter."

Alan: I'm still struggling with that idea of being a messenger or an angel. I guess my discomfort comes as I reflect back on the number of years that perhaps I had the message in the form of my own story of what had happened to me, and the number of years that I resisted even mentioning any part of that story. You ask, "Do you want to be an angel? Do you want to be a messenger?" Part of me says, "No." I don't want to tell this story which challenges not only . . . it doesn't challenge the assumptions about who I think I am because I know who I am, but it would certainly challenge the assumptions of who people might think I am. And so the idea of being a messenger or an angel is a very uncomfortable idea. I don't know if I want to do that. Are any of the rest of you uncomfortable?

Linda: It's just also sometimes I think, Alan, that there may have been an attempt to try to be a messenger that was not well received.

Jack: Well, it's not going to be well received because his message, the message of his story, is, like you say, it's partly about who you are – and that's fine because you got that figured out – but the message is also about who your hearers are; and they will kill you before they hear that – or at least that's the perception.

David: According to this message, they won't be Jacob anymore, they'll be Israel; too. They'll know.

Jack: Ah – because the message about who they are is that they sent you out to be who you were.

Harvey: Since I seem to be an advocate of the idea here. Russ and I perhaps excepted – that the people here are messengers. First you reluctance is certainly very familiar. Socrates didn't want to go out and do his examinations in his philosophical inquiries. Of course, Mohammed negotiated with Allah when Allah said, "You know, you're going to be my messenger." And Mohammed said, "Thank you. I really want to thank you for that. That's very thoughtful and I'm so honored, but there are many . . . I got a business, I got a job!" He was a prosperous merchant and he said. "There are many people more qualified than I." And God said, "No, you don't get it. You don't pick this job; I pick you for this job." And so you're in good company in that regard. Number one. Number two, as a thought for consideration, please consider that the actual stories of the people here in country are so extreme that I think many people would not be prepared to hear them. For me, I am supremely honored to be allowed to hear them, but that's who I am. On the other hand, one of the things that I've been struggling with is that I've never had a good or on-going relationship until now with a person of the clergy. And I look at other people too, and the clergy are kind of remote. They're seen as different, kind of exalted and mysterious – I don't know if I'm the only one . . .

Charlie: That's one way of putting it. But the exalted and mysterious - I see the dark side of that.

Harvey: What is interesting, what's powerful about the messengers in this community that these are the messengers that I would go to for spiritual support, not so much to say, though I profoundly eager to hear your stories, but I could go to any one of you and say I am in sorrow, trusting you as a messenger, and so maybe it doesn't relate directly to your experiences in country but it is a taking of those experiences as a catalyst changing that toxin into something that can help other people. That what it means to be a angel – to come down from heaven down to earth – or in this case to go from hell towards heaven. You don't have to go that high up towards heaven. I'm not that close. The messages you can give, they can just be on a regular level; but the clergy, the organized clergy, as a group, are not people I can turn to for support. And I don't know many people, lay people out there, who can turn to clergy – they turn to psychologists, psychiatrists, friends, alcohol, drugs . . .

Charlie: Bartenders.

Harvey: Bartenders?

Charlie: That's what one of my deacons told me. He said he heard more religion Saturday night in the bar than he did in church on Sunday morning.

Harvey: Well, there you are. And I think you might be willing to accept that form of "messenger-ship" a little more. And by the way, I don't know if what I'm saying is correct.

Jack: The other side of what you're saying is I think for me – my acculturation – and I know it's wrong and it's very powerful – the acculturation that if I'm just able to convince you about how knowledgeable I am and how powerful I am and how religious I am that you will like me and respect me and feel comfortable with me and so forth. And I know that's bullshit, but it's still my acculturation. And I will still do it at the drop of a hat.

Harvey: But you know what's so cool about you is that you dropped out of the itinerancy because you know it's bullshit. That role, if you were to do it in that way, you would know it would not be being a true messenger; so you dropped out of it. You're here; you're doing many things of deep value. So good. You're fine. You're cool.

Jack: Well, I'm venturing out into the deep water at this point because since 1971 I have never taken a dollar for any church-like thing that I've done. People will pay me for a wedding occasionally or something, and I will send it on to the seminary or something. I'll give it away. I don't want it. O.K. I've just put myself in a position where I am going to accept a dollar for doing something which comes out of certainly my secular skills and so forth but it comes out of my being back in a position of ministry, and that scares me.

Harvey: Brother, I understand your concern because I have a feeling that you and I are going to traveling that path together. Your adventure in that and the courage that is involved in that has not escaped me.

Ken: Can I ask you a question, Alan? When you came to the meeting in Des Plaines and told your story, for the first time?

Alan: Yes.

Ken: We saw you as somebody that opened up things. What did you see us as?

Alan: When I came to what was the Second Conference meeting, in the Chicago area, I had no idea what to expect, but I was so desperate – and maybe desperation is an aspect of being a messenger – I was so desperate to find anything that would help me put myself back together. And I came there looking for people who would kind of glue me back together, and what I got were people who would sit around in a group, like this, and they would tell stories about what had made them who they were – in relationship to the war – and I sat there, and some of the stories were incredible stories of pain and anguish and courage – I sat there listening – being very quiet, not saying very much of anything – and I was jealous. I thought to myself, "Well, these guys are story-tellers. Maybe there's some hope for me, but I don't think so because I haven't got anything that I want to say about who I am and why I got to be that way." And as I look back upon that experience, and what happened then, after I did tell my story, after that son of a bitch Phil set me up . . .

John: You mean that angel!

Alan: Yeah. That angel. That son of a bitching angel!

Harvey: He is very angelic.

Jack: Cherubic.

Alan: Looking back, what the group was to me, individually and as a group, they were somehow angels or messengers, and having heard their particular stories that related to who they were - and the wrestling that went on in somehow bringing them into some sort of integrated lifestyle where they were in the United

States, living back home in America, and who they had been overseas - that wrestling process gave me a bit of hope; but I had no way to act on that hope until I was able to articulate portions of my story that troubled me, that I thought were unacceptable, that I kept hidden and at a distance. I always think of that group – that particular meeting – in terms of a moment of great grace, because all of a sudden I spoke about what I did in country, the losses that I perceived, and you didn't turn me out. I fully expected, you know, here I've told this story and now everybody rises up in righteous indignation and kills me – and nobody did – and in my own mind, I deserved to die. And maybe at that conference, that part of me did. It's almost like you come to the end of that story where Jacob saw the face of God. That's the face of the messenger – the face of God. That could be a whole bunch of different faces. I could argue that the faces of the people at that conference – individually and collectively – were the face of God; just as I could argue, I think, as well that when I went to the conference with Thich Nhat Hanh, I encountered the face of God.

Jack: I just had an image, as you were talking about the experience of facing the group, having told your story, and expecting now they were going to kill you, of Isaac up there on the altar waiting for his father's hand to strike him. And then the experience of the hand not being there. It's almost as if somebody pulled the ram out from the thicket and there you were with the group. I don't know if that works completely, but that image came to my mind.

Alan: What we did do at that point was a communion service -- more or less – so in a way, the ram was pulled out of the thicket.

Ken: My memory of that time is you scared the shit out of me. I didn't know whether to walk away or to hug you. That was, I think, in many ways, that conference in all of its humor and sadness and pain really glued the group together. I think you were the catalyst for us at that time, others at other times. Looking back on it, that's why I asked you how you saw us. I didn't feel like an angel, but I've never forgotten it. I never will.

Linda: To find "The Lord is this place and I did not know it." Rarely do we know it at the time; acknowledgment comes only after the fact.

John: I think that says something about trying to find a way to turn this experience into an opportunity, which I agree is damn hard, but I think that it happens here. Not without a great deal of a pain and struggle, but there's something about . . . I don't know all the terms . . . but the witnessing. You could have said that to, you know, a sociology class, and it wouldn't have nearly the weight; but saying it to this group and us having the privilege of hearing it, the privilege and the pain of hearing it . . . was . . . had a lot of meaning.

Russ: You know, the ministry that I have taken from this conference is the facilitator of telling of stories with the Vietnam veteran that I see, when I look, when I know the history of how this conference came into being, you are the chief facilitator of the telling of all of our stories because you are a very special angel to this conference.

John: I'm not sure what you mean.

Russ: You are the one who facilitated Phil's story. And from that this conference was born!

Alan: You're the angel of this conference.

Jack: John's the granddaddy of all angels!

John: I was just going to offer as aside that I cringe every time that Phil tells the story. It's . . .

Harvey: Does everybody know the story? Because I don't.

Linda: Yes, you do.

Harvey: I do know it? O.K.

Linda: Phil said it yesterday. He was at that conference and this guy came up to him and said, "Are you all right?"

Harvey: Oh!! You're the guy!

Alan: There's a good deal of discomfort, I think, I hearing someone say you were a messenger or an angel at some particular point because we are used to the image of angels as bright, white lights and good; on the other hand, you've got the dark angel – and if anybody says to me, "You're an angel." I immediately assume that I'm the dark angel.

Ken: Or that they're full of crap.

Alan: Yeah. Or that they're full of crap.

Jack: Or both.

Alan: Because if you want to talk about the "angelic" work that we did in country, well that leaves me . . . I was the angel of death. That was what I did. And to hear that there might be something positive coming out of that, it forces me to begin to re-think things, and nobody likes to re-think things like that, to put aside things that you have become used to, if not comfortable with. You know, I became very used to, for years, having uncontrollable flashes of rage. When they finally stopped, after I began to work on my story and to claim a portion of the grace of healing, well, after they stopped, damn it, I missed them! Because I was so used to them. I'd go so far as to, every now and then, sit down and say, "I need a good flash of rage." And, damn it, I couldn't summon it up! I'd lost it. It had been taken away.

Jack: You got wounded.

Alan: Yeah.

Ken: In your hip, and you've been limping ever since.

Alan: Yeah. That's something else.

Ray: One of the things that Russ and I were talking about last night is the fact that the message, the historical message, in many of the text books which our children, or our children's children, are reading, as was reported on a news broadcast not recently, they were doing a critique of what students study about history. Vietnam, the story of Vietnam, received one page. And Marilyn Monroe got thirteen pages. Now I mean what does that say about not only those who fought, and those who lived, and those who died, but what does it say about our society as a culture? And what it is or who is it that's shaping the future? Albeit aside from we as individuals who are called to serve that high authority, as angels, as messengers, as whatever. I mean when you sit in a room of a person who is dying and the best that you can do is hold that person's hand and to, as I have phrased it to family members, celebrate this time in which you walk that person to that doorway and hand that person off into the hand of God, without saying a word, but just being present. But what does it say about those who are telling the story to our children's children who are reading one page about the history of the war in Southeast Asia, which was the longest war in our history, or the thirteen pages about Marilyn Monroe? Something – How does the expression go - something is rotten in Denmark. Something really stinks.

Charlie: Besides the fish.

Ray: Yeah. Besides the fish.

Charlie: You know the dark side of that is when I was a young person in Vietnam, I probably would have been more interested in the thirteen pages of Marilyn Monroe that reading about some damn war because I would know what I was reading would be all bullshit anyway.

Jack: But you wouldn't have believed the thirteen ages about Marilyn Monroe was bullshit, and I'll bet those thirteen pages didn't get anywhere close to what a wounded person she was.

Ray: No.

Harvey: Going back briefly to the angel or messenger idea, I just want to emphasize that in my mind, in terms of the check list for angels, in addition to those who don't want to accept the mission - that's one of the things - another check for an angel is that there would be kind of a not wanting to accept the mission, but saying, "I'm not an angel – you're an angel." And I just saw that happen around here. It was going, "No . . .no . . . no . . .you!" Everybody was pointing the finger; it's another part of the checklist. Then the last thing I would say is that I think it is clearly the case that angels or messengers do cover a wide spectrum from the very, very dark and diabolical to luminous and very, very bright. Maybe it is the mission of every messenger or angel to try to move towards the light, but it is so interesting and so unpredictable, and ultimately I think a matter of divine inspiration, as to what can operate as something that triggers or acts as an igniter of the message.

Linda: Maybe it's both of those occurring at once.

Charlie: The popular cultural view of the angels is this warm, luminous stuff, and I know if I'm wrong Russ will correct me, but it seems to me most of the biblical encounters I remember were real terrifying for the folks who experienced them, not pleasant.

Alan: And perhaps part of the reluctance is we don't want to be the people who bring terror. If you look at it sort of like that, I know that doesn't appeal to me. I've been there, done that! I don't know if I want to do that again.

Harvey: On the angel front – I'm on a roll here – the . . .

Charlie: Why don't you finish that checklist so the angels can get clearance from the tower and fly? I'm still stuck in the mud. My landing gear is bogged down in the mud.

Harvey: There's a . . . I can't remember exactly the context of it, Ray, but you were talking about that experience of catching your daughter as a small child and I think I heard myself saying that was an angel or a blessing. But the concept was that this was angelic. The fact that you had gone through what you had gone though relates to the quality for your catch. You didn't have to tell her about – maybe some day you will -- but I think the way in which you catch her, the way in which you encourage her to jump into your arms, is part of the message process. And that brings me to an anecdote I would like to relate, which has to do with symphonic music. Stravinsky's *Rite of Spring,* when it was first played in Paris, was very controversial, and, in fact, I'm told, a riot actually broke out because the music was so unusual. And the opening note is a high, plaintive held note – a single note by an oboe – a very high note. According to the story the oboist went to Stravinsky and "Maestro," – he was a reluctant messenger – "Maestro, the opening of this symphony, the note, is above the register of the oboe, as I'm sure you know, and I'm wondering if you might rather re-assign it to a reed instrument within whose register it naturally resides?" Stravinsky said, "No, I don't want to." "But Maestro, I can't be sure, I can't be confident that I can hit that note!" And Stravinsky said, "That's it. I want to hear the uncertainty in the performance." I think that all of the stories, all of the experiences that is gathered here may come out directly in its expression in verbal form in the sharing of the stories, but it may come out in the uncertainty or the ambivalence or the anguish or the other feelings that I won't even begin to characterize as you all disperse and affect people.

Home?

Excerpts from the Joseph story in Genesis 39 and 41 (NRSV)

Now Joseph was taken down to Egypt and Potiphar, an officer of the Pharaoh, the captain of the guard, an Egyptian, bought him from the Ishmaelites who had brought him down there. The Lord was with Joseph, and he became a successful man; [he found favor in his master's sight; and Potiphar made him overseer of his house . . .]

Now Joseph was handsome and good-looking. And after a time his master's wife cast her eyes on Joseph and said, "Lie with me." But he refused and said to his master's wife, "Look, with me here, my master has no concern about anything in the house, and he has put everything he has in my hand. He is not greater in this house than I am, nor has he kept back anything from me except yourself, because you are his wife. How then could I do this great wickedness, and sin against God?" And although she spoke to Joseph day after day, he would not consent to lie beside her or to be with her. One day, however, when he went into the house to do his work, and while no one else was in the house, she caught hold of his garment, saying, "Lie with me!" But he left his garment in her hand, and fled and ran outside. When she saw that he had left his garment in her hand and had fled outside, she called out to the members of her household and said to them, "See, my husband has brought among us a Hebrew to insult us! He came in to me to lie with me, and I cried out with a loud voice . . He left his garment beside me, and fled outside." Then she kept his garment by her until his master came home . . .

When his master heard the words that his wife spoke to him, saying, "This is the way your servant treated me," he became enraged. And Joseph's master took him and put him in prison, the place where the king's prisoners were confined . . . But the Lord was with Joseph and showed him steadfast love; he gave him favor in the sight of the chief jailer . . .

After two whole years, Pharaoh dreamed that he was standing by the Nile, and there came up out of the Nile seven sleek and fat cows . . . then seven other cows, ugly and thin, came up out of the Nile after them . . . The ugly and thin cows ate up the seven sleek and fat cows. And Pharaoh awoke. Then he fell asleep and dreamed a second time; seven ears of grain, plump and good, were growing on one stalk. Then seven ears, thin and blighted by the east wind, sprouted after them. The thin ears swallowed up the seven plump and full ears. Pharaoh awoke, and it was a dream. In the morning his spirit was troubled; so he sent and called for all the magicians of Egypt and all its wise men. Pharaoh told them his dreams, but there was no one who could interpret them to Pharaoh. The chief cupbearer said to Pharaoh . . . "Once Pharaoh was angry with his servants, and put me and the chief baker in custody . . . A young Hebrew was there with us, a servant of the captain of the guard. When we told him, he interpreted our dreams for us . . . " Then Pharaoh sent for Joseph, and he was hurriedly brought out of the dungeon. When he had shaved himself and changed his clothes, he came in before Pharaoh. And Pharaoh said to Joseph, "I have had a dream, and there is no one who can interpret it. I have heard it said of you that when you hear a dream you can interpret it."

Joseph answered Pharaoh, "It is not I; God will give Pharaoh a favorable answer . . . "

Joseph said to Pharaoh, "Pharaoh's dreams are one and the same; God has revealed to Pharaoh what he is about to do . . . There will come seven years of great plenty throughout the land of Egypt. After them there will arise seven years of famine, and all the plenty will be forgotten in the land of Egypt; the famine will consume the land . . . Now therefore let Pharaoh select a man who is discerning and wise, set him over the land of Egypt . . . Let them gather all the food of these good years that are coming, and lay up grain under the authority of Pharaoh for food in the cities, and let them keep it. That food shall be a reserve for the land against the seven years of famine that are to befall the land . . ." So Pharaoh said to Joseph, "Since God has shown you all this, there is no one as discerning and wise as you. You shall be over my house . . ." Removing his signet ring from his hand, Pharaoh put it on Joseph's hand; he arrayed him in garments of fine linen, and put a gold chain around his neck . . . Thus he set him over all the land of Egypt . . . Joseph was thirty years old when he entered the service of Pharaoh King of Egypt . . . . Joseph had two sons . . . Joseph named the firstborn Manasseh, "For," he said, "God has made me forget all my hardship and all my father's house." The second he named Ephraim, "For God has made me fruitful in the land of my misfortunes."

* * * * *

Participating: Alan, Charlie, David, Ray, Jack, Jeff, John, Linda, Phil, Russ

* * * * *

Alan: This particular section, which is just a taste of Joseph in exile - we all know the other parts of the story I'm sure - but this one ends up – let's start with the last sentence – here is Joseph in exile and he has said, "God has made me fruitful in the land of my misfortunes." If Vietnam was the land of our misfortunes, can we say, with Joseph, that there has been some fruitfulness from that? And if so, what?

Phil: Well, we're here. That's it – for me anyway. Certainly I always talked about how in my own experience – out of a death experience – came life, and out of that experience in Vietnam I'm doing the work that I'm doing, and I think it's unique, and it's God given – and the people that are given to me to talk to - I think there is some fruit and that's my belief. I always say that no matter how bad things are there's a reason for this; it can be used to do some good for somebody.

Linda: It's certainly done a lot of good for the rest of the world, and everybody else who had been traumatized since Vietnam veterans wouldn't shut up and pretend that nothing had happened – with the diagnosis of PTSD and all of the treatments for it that came from that.

Jeff: I can't separate Joseph from what it says in the fiftieth chapter of Genesis, "You intended to harm me but God intended it for good." I think that's Genesis 50:20.

Charlie: When he's talking to his brothers.

Jeff: How when you're faced with that – we talk about what Joseph went through to get where he was – that he knew at that point in time that what had happened to him – they had intended him evil and yet looking back, he could see the hand of God through that, that God had intended everything that happened for good – not that he had arranged it, not that God had done it – but that God had allowed it with the intention of saving many lives. So I can't separate the two. How does that strike me? The experiences make me who I am – and there has been an awful lot of good from my life and a lot of good things in my life, as well as a lot of bad that came from that experience. I am who I am.

Jack: There are a lot of people out there who have not had the Vietnam experience and, as frustrating as I think we have felt the experience to be, I don't think we'd want to trade places with those people who haven't had the experience. We sometimes think of those people as kind of "clueless."

Linda: And those people that remain "clueless" forever.

Jeff: I was just sitting here thinking about first leave coming back, and spending some time with a bunch of the people I grew up in high school with. They were interested in wine, women, song, convertibles, parties, getting laid – and I'm sitting here going, "Get a life!" I'm worried about staying alive and you're worried about getting laid. How much have we grown apart in two years? And that is one of the reasons I stayed in the military, because I found that there was nothing left for me out here.

Linda: I had a similar experience. I had just gotten back and had a party with all my old friends; we just couldn't connect. However, the reality is that as I get older and they get older and have lived more of life and have gone through the normal ups and downs of pain and life's joys and sorrows and the intensity of it all, we've gotten closer again. Suddenly, it's like they caught up. Because I did go to a reunion recently, and we were finally able to communicate about something that mattered, but before that I felt isolated, disconnected. I did mention that – one of the things that happened to me – I discovered those few really silly stories about the dumb stuff that happened; I could tell people those and they would listen. So it was the only way I could have any kind of release and conversation was with those stories; I just got that part of life.

Alan: One of the images that Linda raises is of exile. Joseph was carried off into this far land of Egypt and was put in exile there. We went off to a far land; I don't know about the rest of you, but I've been back in the United States since 1972 and in many ways I still feel that I am in exile. There are very few places in the United States that I feel totally comfortable.

John: A stranger in a strange land.

Alan: Exactly. A stranger in a strange land. And does the experience of the trauma, be it being cast in jail unjustly or whatever, does that kind of experience of trauma mean that the one who is traumatized is forever in exile in some way? Or is there a way home?

Jack: It's interesting. I think all of the characters we've looked at in Genesis over the last couple of days were really away from home. I mean home is Ur of the Chaldea – after that they left there, and each one of them left and moved on someplace else - they were wanderers, and they weren't part of the people they were among. They were among the Canaanites for part of it – now they're down in Egypt and they're not part of it, so that really the whole Genesis experience is being someplace you're not a part of.

Alan: So then we are now to be reconciled to the fact that we are wanderers.

Jack: Works for me.

John: Wanderers of the spirit.

Alan: Sojourners in a strange land.

Charlie: Tent people.

Alan: Tent people; there is actually probably some comfort in that. There is the Old Testament command to the people: "You shall have a special concern for the widow, the orphan, and the sojourner in your midst." Did we then receive somehow an acknowledging that we're sojourners, temporary residents? Does that square with what you expected?

Charlie: When we came back. No, it does not at all! Those

were not the fantasies that kept the hope up.

Alan: What were the fantasies that kept the hope up?

Charlie: Oh, you know: the joyous reunion, the luxury car, the compliant wife.

David: My wife and I planned to go visit Disneyland when I got back, and we did. It was during the summer and they shot off fireworks at night. I hated that. It was just like when the ammunition dump went up. I've gone to Disneyland again, but I've always made it a point to be inside, away from where they were doing that when the time came. It wasn't the same as it was when I was a kid.

John: Never. The quarterbacks publicize these Disneyland trips after the Super Bowl, and in their case it's after a triumph. It didn't work out that way.

Ray: Just on a different spin, and this is at least the Methodist church, the itinerant ministry provides a vehicle, a coping mechanism, so that you are always a wanderer. As I look back over my time in various churches – yes, in part it was the mentality of the church – but it was also my mentality too that said, "After two years, people are getting too close – I'm out of here." And so I'd move on to a new church, and I wouldn't have to get into it, wouldn't have to deal with it, either with their stuff or my stuff. And so if you look at my pastoral record, it shows two years here, two years there, three years here – oops, there's five years – what happened there? Five years in my last parish. It's just that nomadic life.

Linda: It's certainly the tradition of our Dominican order that we are itinerant mendicants, and I believe that part of it is a certain restlessness that I have come to recognize as part of who I was, but by that same token I connect with other people who are restless.

David: Look at the story of the Exodus. It says that they took the bones of Joseph with them, taking him home to bury him at last four hundred years later or whatever the heck it was. That always sort of grabs me because – this isn't profound or inspiring or anything – but somehow it's always been important to me that there's six feet of American dirt that belonged to me, and some day it's mine. And they can't take that one away from me. It's always going to be mine.

Alan: Eventually the people of Joseph do return to their homeland. Are there other themes that strike you in the whole Joseph narrative? Here is a guy who was sold into slavery; he was, if I can term him as such, a second lieutenant who knew it all . . .

Charlie: With a nice clean uniform.

Alan: Yes. With a nice clean uniform

Charlie: FNG for sure.

Alan: And he's younger than everybody else, but he seems to have all the right answers. Did you have any experience of people like that when you were in Vietnam?

Charlie: People would say, "I don't care what you learned in school or the book told you, this is here. This is the way it is."

David: They threw him into a pit. Everybody told me about "fragging" before I got there. So I watched out.

Alan: Joseph spent some time in prison, unable to escape, caught up in what was going on. Anyone want to reflect on that?

Jack: What struck me when I read that particular passage

was the saying that, "The Lord was with Joseph and showed him steadfast love and gave him favor in the sight of the chief jailer." Like singling out the one positive, cool thing out of the experience: that the chief jailer liked him; and kind of glosses over the fact that if we're going to show favor or steadfast love to somebody probably allowing them to be cast in jail is not part of that. So what does that say about God? It certainly fits in with my idea of God being either limited or self-limiting in terms of God's power because God clearly didn't – God showed him steadfast love - but it didn't mean keeping him out of jail, it didn't mean keeping out of the circumstances – it's just, well, he found favor with the jailer and that was nice. God showed him steadfast love. Kind of strange.

Alan: That was enough.

Linda: It was a woman again.

Jack: What?

Linda: It was a woman, a lying woman.

Charlie: A spurned woman.

Alan: A lying, spurned woman.

Linda: A spurned woman who was trying to lie with him.

David: A woman with plenty of power, you may notice, because they took her word for it right away.

Linda: Well, yeah, we kind of got caught in that lie, didn't we? I mean we're going to Vietnam and this is going to happen and this is what you're going to do and this is what's going to happen afterward, and then we got back and it said, "No, you awful person, you did this!"

Charlie: "You'll be safer in Vietnam that you will be driving on the freeway in L.A."

Alan: Where did you hear that?

Linda: Yeah, who the heck told you that?

Charlie: I don't know, but I heard it lots of times. Must have been a Fort Gordon lie, or a "Fort Garbage" lie, as some people called it.

David: My favorite one – see – I took ROTC so I could go the way I wanted to, when I wanted to, and so I was delayed until 1970 before I got to Vietnam, later than a lot of folks, not everybody, but a lot of folks, and they kept telling me, "It'll be all over before you have to go . . . it'll be all over.' I heard that every week for a long time until I got my active duty orders which said "for assignment to Vietnam in October, 1970."

Alan: The expectations of the nurturing country. Mother America was going to treat us as she said she was going to treat us. The invitation was given in various phrases: come join me and reap all these benefits. And I know when I arrived in country the honeymoon of expectation must have lasted – somebody said twenty minutes – I think is must have lasted twenty-four hours before I was totally disillusioned, I think it was only two hours before disillusionment began to set in.

Charlie: You were an optimist, weren't you?

Alan: Yes, I was kind of an optimist. I was sort of convinced that we could still pull this one out if we all tried.

Charlie: You didn't have any thought about asking the stewardess if you could hide in the latrine so you could sneak back?

Alan: No. Part of the Joseph story deals with dreams . . . anybody want to touch that one?

David: It's dreams that get him into trouble and it's dreams that get him out of trouble. He dreams about their sheaves bowing down to him and all that stuff.

Linda: I don't know that my dreams did anything except get me into trouble.

Russ: The dreams that I pay attention to are the ones when I come to the bed of a veteran patient. I say, "How old are you?" "Fifty years old." "Did you have combat?" "Yes." "Do you have nightmares?" And it's that quick that I can get to their reality. The dream is -- their particular dream -- the one that is the opening, an opportunity to hear who they are, and tell their own exile story. So it's not a pretty dream. These dreams can get to be indefensible – so the dreams are important to me, not because they're all pleasant, but they are an opening.

Alan: Anyone else want to touch that one?

David: From my anthropological past, there's a real interesting book – about the Ohlone Indians – a local native tribe – you know Californian Indians were really mellow – they were the original California dreamers because the person who edited all these interviews from long before with the Ohlone people said it's really tough to get a description of their everyday life because they, in their very enclosed little world, everybody's life was pretty much the identical. What they always wanted to talk about were their dreams because to them that was what was the real reality, the interesting stuff, because they traveled in their dreams; they had interesting things happen in their dreams. So they found dreams as a reality almost more real than their waking reality. Which, I think, for a lot of veterans is exactly how it feels, not a pleasant reality but more real than the awake.

Linda: I think that was part of the reason I drank as much as I did. I discovered when I was drinking I didn't dream – or if I did I wasn't aware of them – so I made them go away.

Charlie: I think I had more trouble with dreams in country but as far as graphic, Technicolor dreams in country when I dreamed I was home – in Technicolor – I woke up smelling the smells of home and we weren't in Kansas any more Dorothy. Aw shucks – I thought I was home

David: It was a burning 55-gallon drum of shit.

Charlie: The trick is not to go after the burning.

Ray: Then you look at some of the ways, the methods, the hallucinogens used to produce dreams which some people, some Native Americans use to make the dreams . . . and to see something much greater.

Phil: I don't know. I really have a hard time relating to this because I know I dream; I just can never remember any of my dreams. But they generally are not unpleasant they're just nondescript. I wake up and I don't have a clue; but I know I dreamed. I mean – even in Vietnam – you were saying you remember your dreams in Vietnam – I can't even remember what I ate for lunch much less what I dreamt in Vietnam. I don't know if I dreamed or not. I must have.

Charlie: It was S.O.S. Or something in a can.

Phil: I always doctored it up. I made gourmet C-rations.

Russ: One of the things that has startled me about dreams is that they are so repetitive and so dreadful that some people will attempt not to sleep, but will attempt to get by on maybe two hours of sleep a night so that they will not run the risk of having dreams. That's a fact – that's a certain reality too.

John: Well, they're still afraid.

Charlie: I've been on the low end of that. Keep on going; stay up until I'm really just exhausted so I'm going to go to sleep.

Linda: Because then you come to bed hoping maybe you've pushed it away?

Charlie: I'm not going to go till I'm really, really sleepy.

Russ: Well, I can do that but that's not what I'm talking about.

Charlie: No, that is the low-end reaction; you're talking about the high end when they go twenty-two hours a day.

Russ: No, I'm talking about dreams so terrible that they do not want to run the risk of having them.

Ray: I've said to my wife, "I hate the nights, I don't want to go to sleep because . . ." And it's funny; it's almost like you know it's going to be one of those night – so you kind of place it upon yourself – you get that – it's sort of like that feeling that you're walking into an ambush, that sixth sense that you are somehow in harm's way – and she'll say to me, "Come to bed!" and I'll say, "I don't want to!" "You're going to fall asleep in the chair." I say, "So what!"

Russ: Does she know the fear that you facing?

Ray: Yeah. I've shared with her the dreams and all, and her sense is to pull me closer and hold on tight.

Russ: Is that to comfort you and keep you from dreaming?

Ray: I suppose so, or that's what she's feeling.

Russ: To keep you from having the dream?

Ray: Or comfort me in that dream. And my response is, "Don't hold onto me." . . . Because I'm afraid of what might happen.

Russ: You might hurt her.

Jack: It's not safe.

David: Some things have to be done by oneself else worse things happen.

Ray: And it can be said that you're retreating to a place of safety. For me it's the deck of our apartment where I can back myself into the corner and I can see everything going on, but people can't see me because we had these big overflowing plants that provided cover – until the frost hit – I was out there one night and people were moving in, still moving in at 3 o'clock in the morning. They had no idea, they didn't know I was there – they were making all kinds of weird remarks about what was going on – and I felt like saying, "Hello there!" but I felt safe because that could not see me, but I could see them through the brush.

Alan: That's a point. In a land of exile, or if you feel in exile - even if it's your land - you need a place of safety, and maybe Joseph expected his master's house to be a place of safety; obviously it wasn't. Do we deceive ourselves when we thing we can have places of safety?

Jack: If so, we keep doing it again and again.

Ray: And that in and of itself becomes a dependency.

Jack: What?

Ray: You want to depend upon that which you have defined for yourself as being safe, or feeling safe.

John: I don't know what I'd do without a place of safety. And sometimes they don't pan out or they're not reliable, but a lot of time they are.

Alan: The illusion of success works for you?

John: Yeah.

Jack: I thing we need to invest in places of safety, places that we can trust, and sometimes that trust is betrayed, as it was betrayed for Joseph here in Potiphar's house; but I don't think that makes it bad for us to seek out places of safety. I don't think it make us co-dependent. I think one of the things we value about this group is that it's a place of safety, and we're all human beings and if we hang out long enough together then probably somebody will end up being betrayed in one fashion or another, but it's still probably the best show in town as far as safety in concerned.

John: Sometimes it feels safer than others.

Jack: Yeah. Yes. One of the things that resonates with me about this story is that Potiphar's home situation and two things really impinge on my Vietnam experience. The very first one was the breakup of my marriage several months before I went into Vietnam, which was a betrayal situation where my wife got down there to Fort Eustis among all the soldiers and it was like going to a candy store. And, looking back at that with the perspective of thirty years, that probably gave me this wonderful aura of safety through Vietnam because I went to Vietnam numb. I went through Vietnam expecting to be killed. I went through Vietnam wanting to get killed. I went though Vietnam probably not wanting to go back. And I really have to get into other people's stories to get into this "Well, I expected a welcome home and nobody met me with parades or anything!" Because then I kind of knew the welcome I was going to get when I went home, and I'd been putting it off for a year. I see that there. Then the betrayal in Potiphar's home, and then the experience this past spring when I let myself get really hooked into this place of safety with this job that I was in. And this is the kind of the first group of people that I've worked with in thirty years who were really doing something that was socially useful, socially important, and they're non-profit organizations and all doing good things so this is really a more safe place for me than the normal business corporation that I've been working with - you know - and them one day they come in and say, "Well, hey, it's been a nice three years, but you're gone. We found somebody else that suits us just a little bit better." Yes, I get with Potiphar's home there.

Russ: Potiphar's wife seems to be a bit friendly.

Jack: Yeah. And even the fact that in this particular case you can read the story as a story of Joseph's uprightness, and Joseph saying, "How could I do this terrible wickedness against God and everything else?" and though this particular "lie with me" scene never takes place, it doesn't change the fact that Potiphar's wife betrayed her husband by making the offer, betrayed Joseph by screwing his position in that house, betrayed by taking some place that should have been a place of safety and making it a place that wasn't safe at all.

David: He was a straight arrow though all and that's what got him in big trouble. He did everything he thought he was supposed to do, and that's why he ended up in the slammer.

Jack: Although if he'd gone along with it, I'm not sure that would have guaranteed his longevity.

Linda: Until she got tired of him.

Jack: That'd be a no win situation.

John: And then he would have been in jail anyway.

Linda: But I agree with David there is a certain sense of the expectation that if you do the right thing and if you continue to do the right thing, then everything is going to be all right and the reality is that it's not that at all.

David: You'd better do right because you like doing right because it is probably all the reward you'll get.

Russ: I was reflecting on my orders to Vietnam. Vietnam may seem like an exile but it was a reprieve, a restful reprieve from a very troublesome marriage which has since ended up in divorce and failure – but what a relief! I looked forward to this time to be much quieter than the chaos that I knew so well– and that was true all the time I was there – I wasn't in a dangerous situation, so it really was not an exile for me at all in the sense that it was for the rest of you.

Linda: I didn't feel the exile there; I felt the exile when I returned.

Russ: But as we look at it the way we approached our different, our interpretations, exile could be a different exile than what I left – exile is what I returned to.

Linda: I wonder how many chaplains were running away from bad wives?

Jack: Well, we've got four in this group and we're running at fifty percent.

John: The other two haven't said.

Alan: Well, Ken's a priest.

Linda: Maybe it was some experience with bad sisters, and

Charlie's just not saying anything.

Phil: The whole exile thing – I don't relate well with it either because I had an unusual situation when I came home, I came home to a very loving family. There was only the three of us, so there was nothing very big about that – but it was – we were always a very close family and I came back with a job waiting for me because I was drafted out of a job and so that was guaranteed when I came back and they were all . . . it was a wonderful company to work for – they were all very supportive of me while I was over there – they used to – the office – send me food packages and letters and I mean they were just like family. They were an insurance company, home-based in Wisconsin so they had that mentality - even in Los Angeles – Employer's Insurance of Wausau – so when I came back I went back to work for them, and it was wonderful and they treated me like a hero, but the only thing I really remember that was slightly negative was when they asked me how it was and I began to tell them, then they'd say, "That's nice; we're glad you're back." And that's it. You could tell that you could only go a certain distance with them.

John: How about your family?

Phil: My mother, my father, they didn't want to hear anything about it. They were just glad I was home. But I never wanted to tell them anyway. But the thing was that was O.K. Because I was perfectly willing to resume a normal life and forget that year. It fed into my wanting to swallow things and my good nature and optimistic view of life and just forget that it ever happened and I thought it would always go away and stay away. But it didn't; it surfaced in a very strong fashion in 1983 when I entered into a therapeutic relationship at the VET Center; but up to that point it was a very, very good life – superficial – I mean I never let myself go very deep and I didn't let myself get hurt or I didn't let anybody close to me – only to a certain point – so I was in kind of a dream-like state, I guess, not real but it kept me happy anyway.

Linda: My best friend from high school, Margaret, when we got together – she was at the University of Santa Clara at this time – was telling me about some of the anti-war protests that were coming up, and so I started to tell her about some of my experiences, to support what they were doing, and she cut me off before I even got to the second paragraph and said, "We don't want to hear any of that. Anything that happened to you, you deserved, because you wanted to go!" And that was my best friend! Thus ended the friendship.

Charlie: Your best friend?

Linda: Yeah. I haven't seen her since.

Ray: Two things come to mind. Number one: as you spoke, Phil, and also as you spoke. While I was in Vietnam I sent home every penny from my paycheck except for twenty dollars. Now granted twenty dollars would get you quite a bit in Vietnam, a carton of cigarettes was about a buck forty-five. If I got into a poker game I promised myself I would spend no more than five bucks. If I won five bucks, I'd put the five bucks back in my pockets and keep on playing. I got home and what do I discover? Every dime that was sent home was spent on my wife's mother's habit. Boy, was I pissed! Secondly, the other thing that came to mind, most recently since all this came out, we got together for my aunt's 89th birthday – her sister-in-law, my aunt by marriage, her son Jack who had been a marine in between wars and spent his time charging the beaches of Hawaii . . .

David: Some people have a great sense of timing, don't they?

Ray: Yeah. And so he said, "So how are you doing?" And I

said, "Well, not too . . .." And he said, "That's enough about that Vietnam shit. I don't want to hear anymore about that stuff.' And I felt like saying, "Fuck you." I'm sorry, but he didn't want to get below that; he didn't want to know.

John: Very few people did.

Linda: My brothers and sisters and my mother, we've had very little conversation. What's curious is that my niece and nephews ask a lot. They really want to know. And they handle it well. My niece when she was in college and was doing a report on this, we got into some pretty definite things and she sat there, tears coming down her face, but she stayed in there with it all the way though. What was interesting was before, when she said, "I really need to you to talk with me and tell me what happened." And I said, "Sally, you're just too young for this!" She said, "Linda, I'm twenty-two. I'm two years older than you were when you went through it! Talk to me." And I was, like, "Oh, yeah, right. O.K." But I've found among my nieces and nephews there's a lot more genuine caring.

Harvey: I find that also with the kids. With thirteen year olds and my thirteen year old son. One of the things that we did in our area in Southern California was when one of the moving Walls was there. There was a unit - the 199th – and I've been in contact with a veteran of the 199th and the arrival of the wall coincided with the 30th anniversary of the day on which this soldier was gravely wounded. So what we did, we were volunteering at the Wall, and we decided to do because he lives in Philadelphia was a tribute in kind of celebration that he's doing well and doing good things and we read from some of his poetry and did some other stuff and I dragooned some of my son's friends to attend along with the family – one guy in particular – a wonderful young man – did the video – because we sent a video – he wanted a video sent back – which we did – and whenever I see him he says. "Let's do it again – let's do it again!" And then, back in school, he said, "My social science teacher is a Vietnam veteran. Could you talk to him?" Maybe the passage of time beings some hope with it.

Linda: You know something. It wasn't just us. Everybody, the whole nation, was wounded.

Harvey: I agree with that.

Russ: The people that you talked to, that you shared with us, that's remarkable that you can do that because a recent experience I had when I saw a movie, which I think, was about Vietnam trauma. It was in a religious setting and so I said, "I think this is about Vietnam." And they began to say, "Well, you're a nice chaplain . . ." And they went on to theologize and categorize and all these other things. And I was furious because this is like saying, "We know the deeper meaning of what's here; you don't know. What you say doesn't matter!" Next day I went down to that minister's office and I said, "This was about Vietnam and trauma! And let me tell you, I deal with this when I work." And so he knew I was madder than a wet hornet. So, in other words, it was wonderful that you had such a reception from a certain set of people that you told your story to, but as recently as four or five weeks ago, this is what I got!

Linda: No, I get that from my sisters in community. I'm running into that problem now with sisters in the community. It's nice to have someone.

Jack: I wonder if it's a pattern that it – like our generation of people who weren't there are the ones who are absolutely closed off to it – and somehow there's this opening in the next generation down – your nephews and nieces – I had this experience upon the internet a year ago where I got this e-mail from a fifteen or sixteen year old girl somewhere in Ohio. She's found some of my poetry on my internet site and she wants permission to read it in her high school speech class and I say, "Go ahead. O.K. That's cool." Then I get another note that says, "My speech instructor says if I'm going to do that I need to find out something about you. Can you tell me something about your experience." But as she very quickly rushed on to say, "But you don't have to say anything if it's too painful or something." And it was just so touching to be taken care of by this sixteen year old!

John: I speak in a lot of different schools about PTSD and the war and usually I'll bring a vet with me, another vet, and the kids generally are riveted and they're so into it, particularly the kids that are close to the age that we were when we went. Because we tell them, we weren't that much older and how would you feel? How would your reaction be? What would you be doing, be thinking? And you can see them.

Alan: Perhaps we're at the point where we can say that we're at the place where we started, and maybe there's a little bit of light and hope. With luck, or through grace, we may be able to, some day, fully witness to that truth spoken at the end of the passage, "God has made me fruitful in the land of my misfortunes."

* * * * *

More About the Moderator

Alan Cutter grew up in a pastor's family in Massachusetts, spending long summers at the family home in Southern Maine. Following in his Father's footsteps, he became a pastor, but only after serving on active duty in the US Navy for five years. This included a tour of duty in Vietnam. His pastorates were in Maine, New York, West Virginia and Minnesota; his last call was to be a church executive in South Louisiana following the trauma of hurricanes Katrina and Rita. When he was diagnosed with Agent Orange-related Parkinson's Disease in 2010, having previously been diagnosed with post-traumatic stress disorder, he retired. Alan has earned the following degrees a Bachelor's in English, (Syracuse, 68), a Master's in Library Science (Simmons, 70), a Master of Divinity (Bangor Seminary, 77) and a Doctor of Ministry (Pittsburgh, 96). The first two years of his military service were as an enlisted man going to various schools and studying North Vietnamese at the Defense Language Institute in Monterey, California. In late 1971, following his commissioning as an Ensign, he was sent directly to Vietnam, where he worked in and around Danang. While a member of the National Conference of Viet Nam Veteran Ministers, he edited the Vietnam Veterans of America Book of Prayers and Services. He has co-led numerous veterans' retreats on Trauma and Spirituality, spoken at the International Society of Traumatic Stress Studies, and been a consultant with the Canadian Armed Forces working with units deploying to Afghanistan. Currently he is president of the International Conference of War Veteran Ministers. He is married to Ann, who acts as his editor.

Visit Alan's webpage: http://amazon.com/author/alancutter

Ann Cutter grew up in Maryland where her father was a civilian employee of the U.S. Army at Edgewood Arsenal. She attended the University of Delaware, earning Bachelors and Masters Degrees in American Studies. Alan and Ann have three children and four grandchildren.

Our books are available through Amazon:

At the Altar of War is a novel. **God's Story, My Story** and **An Alphabet of God, War, and Hope** are books of meditations. **Hope and Healing for Veterans** describes the retreats that he helped lead for veteran and partners. **The Letter of Paul to the Beloved Warrior** is the book that "should be" in the Bible.

The Land of My Misfortunes